The Golden Age of
Cork Cinemas

John McSweeney

Rose Arch Publications

First Published 2003

Published by
Rose Arch Publications
Rose Arch
Old Blackrock Road
Cork
Email: rosearchpubs@yahoo.co.uk

ISBN No.: 0-9545755-0-4

Printed in Ireland by Litho Press Co., Midleton, Co. Cork.

For my parents Anne and Eamonn,
and my aunt Meta

CONTENTS

AUTHOR'S INTRODUCTION

Growing up, my father regaled me with tales of the days he used to go to the pictures several nights a week. His stories introduced me to the golden era of cinemas in Cork – a world full of unique venues, populated with colourful characters, thrilling films and memorable moments. This world had largely disappeared by the time I arrived on the scene. In my formative years, the cinemas of Cork were in the winter of their lives. Television and videos had taken away a large section of their audience, and these grand old buildings started to look like relics from a bygone age.

In January of 1980, I was taken to my very first film. The picture was *The Muppet Movie* and the cinema was the Palace. This magnificent theatre filled me with an overwhelming sense of awe and wonder. When the lights went down and the picture first appeared on screen, a sense of magic descended on the theatre unlike anything I had witnessed before. As I got older, the lure of cinema continued to work its celluloid charm. Then one week in August of 1989, the industry changed forever when the multiplex arrived in town. The cinemas had moved into the modern age and the days of the individual picture houses had come to an end.

The rich tapestry of social history quickly fades, and individual tales are often lost before someone has had the opportunity to put them down on paper. I did not want that to happen here. This book has been compiled from four years of research, during which time I met with many different people who generously contributed to this history of Cork's old cinemas. I've aspired to reconstruct an accurate account of the picture houses and their personnel, the films and their fans, the city and its characters. I hope it brings back memories to an older generation for whom the past will always retain a special significance, and introduces a younger crowd to a world they never knew.

John McSweeney
August 2003

1. THE FIRST PICTURE SHOW

BEFORE TELEVISION, BEFORE VIDEOS, before the Internet, there was only one place to go for an evening of entertainment and that place was the cinema. No other form of mass entertainment had a greater impact on the world in the 20th Century. They were shrines of public amusement in the Ireland of old, which brought people together and offered them a window on the world. A trip to the pictures was a major social occasion that satisfied everyone's needs, and it provided unparalleled escapism in an age of economic hardship, unemployment and political unrest. The cinema swept people away to far off places, and introduced them to glamorous screen idols, courageous heroes, seductive leading ladies, and demonic villains. Movies added a rich layer of excitement to the lives of their spectators by allowing them to participate in great adventures, thrilling spectacles and whirlwind romances. Of course, the nature of Cork people being what it is, there were always enough characters and smart alecs in the audience to supply live in-house entertainment to go with the picture.

Today all the multiplexes show the same films simultaneously, but back in the golden age of cinema in Cork each house showed different types of pictures, and thereby drew a different clientele. Film goers had a great choice and the more dedicated would go three or four times a week. The Savoy was the finest of all Cork's picture palaces, and along with the Capitol, Pavilion and Palace, provided the latest in big screen attractions in luxurious surroundings. The Coliseum, the Lee and the Ritz often supplied the top features several months after their initial release. Although these houses weren't quite as upmarket as some of their neighbours, they nonetheless pulled in the crowds. Then there were the Assembly Rooms, the Imperial, St. Mary's Hall and the Lido which offered thrilling pictures in admittedly 'modest' surroundings for those who couldn't afford the price of admission to the more exclusive cinemas.

People who lived through those times fondly recollect the colourful and amusing memories that made the period so rich and eventful. No one who sat through Fred Bridgeman's Sunday night sing-a-longs at the Savoy can ever forget what it felt like to be part of a choir of two thousand people. Many a person can recall taking a date to Pav's restaurant for 'high tea' and then going onto the cinema for a feature. Others lovingly hark back to the times when they shouted and cheered at the cowboy films that entertained the younger generations in the Assembly Rooms and the Lido. These picture houses were unique places and everyone has their own reason for remembering them.

The cinemas also fed into the blood of their employees. Many individuals devoted a lifetime of service to the business and look back on their careers with great fondness. Some worked as managers and projectionists, others as ushers, sweet sellers and maintenance men, yet what ever job they held, they took great pride in their work. In several cases, their children and even their grandchildren followed them into the business. People like Johnno in the Savoy, Georgie in the Assembly Rooms, Marky Holland of the Ritz, Michael John O'Sullivan of the Lee, or Donal Kelly of the Pavilion became figures of local legend in Cork. Others like Michael Murphy of the Palace, Dan Williamson of the Savoy and Seamus Quinn of the Cameo worked behind the scenes and out of the public eye, but their contributions to the business were equally immeasurable. This book is the story of the cinemas in Cork as told by their employees and patrons.

THE STORY BEGINS in April 1896 with a fair in aid of the Munster Convalescent Home, held in the Assembly Rooms on the South Mall. This multifunctional premises hosted such diverse events as theatrical shows, political rallies, choral recitals and boxing matches, and it was only fitting that such a venue would have the honour of showing the first film in the city. The festivities, which were organised by Lady Arnott of Woodlands and Miss Reeves from Douglas, consisted of a grand competitive flower show, a military band, and as a special feature of the fair, 'Splendid Living Pictures'. On April 29th, without any fanfare to mark this momentous occasion, the first moving pictures were displayed in Cork. The show was screened four times that day at 3pm and 4pm, and again at 8pm and 9pm, and admission cost the princely sum of one shilling.

The show at the Assembly Rooms took place less than ten days after the very first films were screened in Ireland. On April 20th 1896, Dan Lowrey's Star of Erin Theatre in Dublin presented 'The Cinématographe', which was billed as an immense scientific

The Olympia Theatre, formerly Star of Erin Music Hall, where the first films were shown in Ireland in 1896

3

invention and one of the greatest novelties ever to come to Dublin. Many people crowded into the theatre to see Ireland's first picture show, but a large number left disappointed. Most of the audience couldn't make sense of the indistinguishable images of an acrobat, fighting cats and a Scots drummer which were dancing around on the screen. On that evidence it seemed as if cinema didn't have much of a future, but Dan Lowrey felt differently. Later that year he brought an improved picture show back to his theatre. This time the projection was enhanced and the show became a sensational hit.

The new medium grew steadily in popularity as the technology evolved, and pictures started to become a regular feature on the Cork theatrical circuit by the end of the 19th Century. On September 9th 1896, the Opera House presented "Latest and Greatest Sensation of the London Season – The Animated Photographs Projected by the Marvellous 'Vitagraph' – The Most Perfect and Costly Mechanism yet Invented for this Purpose." The Opera House enjoyed considerable success with this presentation and imported many other film shows from England over the next few years. Such was the demand for these pictures that other venues got in on the act. The City Hall (known at the time as the Municipal Buildings) showed films as part of their Easter Fete Speranza in 1897, while during the same week Dan Lowrey opened his Palace of Varieties on King Street (now MacCurtain Street), and the first show featured 'Professor Jolly's World Renowned Cinématographe.' In the early years of the 20th Century, the Assembly Rooms started holding regular screenings too.

THE FIRST PICTURE house opened in America in 1905, and Ireland's first such venue was the Volta at 45 Mary Street (just off O'Connell Street) in Dublin. It was opened by the Irish writer James Joyce on December 20th, 1909. He had been living in the Italian city of Trieste when he got the idea for the Dublin picture house, and he found a group of Italian cinema owners who were favourable to his proposal. They agreed to put up the money, with the intention of extending the business to Cork and Belfast if the circumstances were right. He left for Ireland in October of 1909, and two months later his plan came to fruition when the Volta commenced business. (Incidentally, it was named after a picture house in Bucharest that was owned by the same Italian group.) Sadly, Joyce's hopes of expanding the business in Ireland were dashed when another team of entrepreneurs started a cinema in Cork seven days after the Volta opened in Dublin. This picture house was The Electric Theatre and was located on Maylor Street. A lessee of The Irish Electric Theatres Ltd, it was operated under the management of Allan S. Davenport and had the telephone number 732.

Billed as 'THE NEWEST AND CHEAPEST ENTERTAINMENT IN THE SOUTH OF IRELAND', The Electric Theatre remained in business for only a very brief period and endured many financial hardships in its short lifetime. Despite that, it occupies a very unique position in the history of Cork in that it can be considered as the first official cinema in the city. Its Grand Opening Matinee on Monday, 27th December, 1909 consisted of 'THREE GREAT THRILLS' – *A Dash for the North Pole, The Derby 1909* (From Start to Finish), and *Nick Carter.* In addition to these spectacles, the opening show featured another film called *The Suffragette's Dream* and, as its notice in The Cork Examiner indicated, 'Also a Host of Other Attractions that Will Interest and Amuse Grave and Gay Alike'. The Stalls at 6d were the most expensive seats in the house, while less extravagant customers could enjoy the more economical comforts of the Pit Stalls for 4d, or the Gallery and Promenade for 2d.

The Electric Theatre ran three shows nightly at 6.15, 7.45 and 9.15, and a lot of filmed entertainment was crammed into the ninety minute period. However within a fortnight of opening it was forced to reduce its nightly shows to just two performances per evening as the operating costs were excessively high. By the end of January 1910 it went out of business temporarily, only to be reopened the following March under the management of Mr. C.F. Fielding. He also owned an engineering and electrical company on the Grand Parade which supplied magic lanterns and other cinematographic material. Second time around the Electric Theatre didn't fare any better, and after an initial success it had closed again by the following April. This time it didn't reopen.

Despite the failure of the Electric Theatre, picture shows continued to feature prominently on the bills of many of Cork's houses of entertainment. The Palace continued to show short films in their weekly Music Hall programme, as did the Assembly Rooms Picturedrome. In October 1912, the committee of St. Mary's Hall opposite the North Cathedral got in on the act by opening the first of their many seasons of films. This parish hall was a long standing favourite for several generations, and in numerous instances it was the place where many a youngster from the Northside saw their first picture. In the same month, the Capuchian owned Fr. Matthew Hall also started exhibiting 'living pictures'. In November of that year, the Tivoli at 21 Merchants Quay was opened by a local business man. Billing itself as 'The Only up-to-date Picture Theatre in Cork', it was a very modern emporium for its time and had a continuous show from 4pm to 11pm daily. The Tivoli was unique in its design features as it guaranteed every patron would get a good view of the images on the screen, regardless of where they were sitting. It also differed from many of the other picture houses as the projector was located in a room separate from the rest of the auditorium.

In February of 1913, the Imperial Cinema on Oliver Plunket Street (then George's Street) became the latest picture house to open in Cork. This cinema, which is best remembered by the nickname Miah's, was a very popular and expensive spot in the early years. However, as time progressed the prices fell and it developed a reputation as Cork's most prominent fleapit. More significantly, 1913 saw the opening of the Coliseum at the corner of MacCurtain Street (then King Street) and Brian Boro Street. The

Col had the honour of being the first custom built cinema in the city. It proved to be a spectacular new entertainment venue, and its popularity endured with the people of Cork over the course of the next fifty years.

When the Tivoli closed in 1915 after just three years in business, a halt was put on the cinema building boom. This closure inhibited financiers from further speculation until 1920, when the economic climate was more favourable to investment again. The first of the new wave of cinemas to open was the Washington on Great George's Street (now Washington Street). The Bellevue Cinema on Military Road opposite the Barracks was the first of the suburban picture houses to open in 1920. Its initial venture into the film business was a success, but it was converted into a dance hall a few years later. However, the Bellevue did enjoy a second spell as a cinema in the 1960s when it was relaunched as the Cameo. The other suburban cinema to open in 1920 was the Blackpool at 70-74 Watercourse Road. This theatre was later renamed the Lido and became a beloved institution for two generations of Northsiders. The following year, at the height of the War of Independence, the Pavilion on Patrick Street opened to great acclaim. The Lee Cinema on Winthrop Street, which had originally been destroyed during the burning of Cork the previous Christmas, received a second lease of life in September 1921.

WHEN MOTION PICTURES were first invented in the late 19th century, very few people could have foreseen the lasting impact they would have on the world. Thomas Edison, who was one of the pioneers of the movie camera, said in 1895 that he doubted "there was any commercial future" for his invention. However, as movie going audiences grew by millions in each of the early years of the 20th century, it was clear that this phenomenon was here to stay. The multitude of cinemas in Cork introduced the movie going masses to all the latest silent films from America, and the local audiences delighted in watching an array of international talent strut their stuff on the silver screen. Stars like Rudolph Valentino, Douglas Fairbanks, Mary Pickford, Greta Garbo, Alice Joyce, John Gilbert, Gloria Swanson and Charlie Chaplin were the matinee idols of their day, and their faces became known throughout the world. A single pianist or violinist provided live music to accompany the films, but some of the more upmarket cinemas splashed out on a string quartet. The Pavilion even had a small orchestra. However, just as silent movies were winning their way into everyone's hearts and minds, an earth shattering event happened in 1927 that changed the world of movies forever: they started to talk.

The technology for sound films had existed since 1900 when Frenchman Leon Gaumont developed a system by which gramophone recordings were synchronised to films of music hall performers. The scheme led to frequent breakdowns, and editing pictures to match the sound and the action became almost impossible. In an age of innovation, many people in America and Europe tried their hand at creating a scheme to make movies speak, but it was not until 1926 that 20th Century Fox designed the first soundtrack. On October 6th 1927, *The Jazz Singer* premiered at the Warner Cinema in New York. When Al Jolson sang 'My Mammy' and 'Toot, Toot, Tootsie, Goodbye', the era of sound was born. That signalled the end of the age of silent films, and many of the old stars had to find new employment as their voices and acting styles did not suit the new medium. The same applied to the musicians, pianists, conductors and other entertainers who provided the live attendant music.

The Leather-Neck, which received its premiere screening in the Opera House on June 11th 1929, was the first sound film to be shown in Cork. The film depicted the adventures of three American Marines and was in fact largely silent. It did however contain unique sound features like marching troops, a café brawl, the firing of machine guns and the voices of its stars William (Hopalong Cassidy) Boyd, Alan Hale, Robert Armstrong and Diane Ellis. The programme was presented by Ireland's most accomplished baritone. Mr. Walter McNally, and the show attracted so many people that the management decided to retain it for a second week. Large numbers of spectators were bowled over by the new technology, while others were disappointed with their first experience of the novelty of sound. Commentators on the event pointed out that the invention was still in its infancy, and like other innovations, its initial shortcomings and flaws would put a lot of people off. After all, the wireless suffered from a similar fate when it emerged some years earlier. It was also mentioned that another new contraption called television was not likely to amaze anyone other than its own supporters in 1929 either. Nonetheless sound films were here to stay, and the ghost of television would return to haunt the cinemas several decades later.

The Pavilion was the first cinema to permanently convert to sound in August 1929, and in the months that followed, the Coliseum, the Lee, and the Washington all installed Western Electric Sound Systems. Clark Gable, Claudette Colbert, Joan Crawford, Gary Cooper and Fredric March among others were the new flavours of the month with audiences everywhere, while many of the superstars of the silent screen were consigned to memory. Sound became a new selling point for cinemas, and the Palace advertised itself as 'The House with the Perfect Sound' in the 1930s. This prompted the Lido in Blackpool to engage in a battle of one-upmanship with its more sophisticated competitor by billing itself as 'The House with the "More" Perfect Sound'.

IN *THE JAZZ SINGER* Al Jolson uttered the words 'You ain't heard nothin' yet', which might have been a prophetic statement signalling that talking pictures were here to stay. In Cork the phrase 'You ain't seen nothin' yet' might have been closer to the point. The Savoy on Patrick Street opened on May 12th 1932, and for over forty years it reigned supreme as the crown jewel of all Cork's picture houses. Seating over 2,200 people, it was the ultimate in luxury, style and sophistication. It was fitted with a stage on which many live acts performed over the years, but the Savoy's most unique and outstanding feature was the impressive Compton organ. On Sunday evening's the organ would rise out of the ground, and Fred Bridgeman would lead the packed crowd in the sing-a-long shows that have now passed into local legend.

The harmony of the set of picture houses was unchallenged for many years, until the Capitol Cinema on the Grand Parade opened on Easter Saturday 1947. Owned by Capitol and Allied Theatres Ltd., Peter Farrell – deputising for the company's manager, his brother Patrick – dedicated the cinema as a monument to Cork, in the hope that it would become central to the life of the city and its people. For many years the Capitol was considered the baby of Cork's cinemas, however Mr Farrell's dedication was prescient in that it is the only one of those original houses that is still operating today. The rest have disappeared with the constant ebb and flow of progress. However in the collective memories of their former employees and patrons, these cinemas continue to endure. The ghosts of the past still survive in the shadows of the mind. It is now time to step back into the days of yore and revisit these picture houses in all their bygone glory.

2. PICTURE PALACES OF DELIGHT

OUR JOURNEY BEGINS with a trip to the four 'first-run' cinemas in Cork. These were top of the range venues where people could catch the biggest Hollywood stars in their latest films. The Savoy, the Pavilion, the Palace, and the Capitol made up the list. If you could afford to go to one of these cinemas on a regular basis you were considered a big shot. They were places to take a girl on a first date, or venues for special occasions. These cinemas were big and spacious, luxurious and commodious, and elegant on a scale that has yet to be equalled in Cork. They had the best films, the best projectors, the most attractive seating, and even the finest toilets. Some had their own restaurants or bars as well. Of course, as they had the best of everything, the prices were of the highest 'standard' too. They were the epitome of the grand movie palaces of yesteryear – the centrepieces of entertainment in any city.

THE SAVOY
Hollywood on Patrick Street

IN THE 1920s, a very refined restaurant called the Savoy opened at 112 Patrick Street. It was one of the more exclusive eating and drinking emporiums in the city, and it even had its own miniature orchestra to play soothing classical music to assist the patrons in digesting their meals. It was the personification of elegance, and only those who could afford its costly prices were privileged to enter and enjoy the services of these elaborate luncheon rooms. However in the early 1930s, construction got underway on an imposing building just four doors down on the same side of the street. When completed, this venue would also operate under the name Savoy and would become the finest place of entertainment in Cork.

The Savoy was commissioned by the Rank Organisation, and built by the firm of Meaghar and Hayes who had also constructed the Savoy Cinema in Dublin. It cost £148,000 to erect, and was completed in just seven months. Joe McCann from Dublin was the foreman on the building and Bertie Hackett, the assistant foreman, later became the cinema's permanent carpenter. In total, one thousand people were employed during the construction phase. The quality of workmanship was of the highest standard as is still evident from the outside today, yet a terrible accident marked the

The Savoy during the construction phase in 1932. Courtesy of Irish Examiner

cinema's beginning. A mason from Cobh named Bill Hogan was one of the people working on the Savoy. One evening as he was building a wall, Mr. Hogan stepped on a mortar board which overturned, throwing him forty feet to the ground and to his death. Tragic as the incident was, the dedicated workmen continued to put in their best efforts, and the day before the building opened, one hundred and forty men from different trades toiled all through the night to ensure that the cinema was completed in time for its grand opening. With the clock ticking away, they managed to finish the bulk of their tasks by 8pm on opening night, although a group of masons were still plastering the projection box while the first film was being shown. That was Thursday, May 12th 1932.

For the previous few days, advertisements on the footnotes of the pages in The Evening Echo printed the words 'START SAYING SAVOY' in big bold letters. The following ad was placed in The Cork Examiner:

Opening on May 12th at 8pm., Savoy Cinema.
Daily 2.30 to 11pm.
Wheeler and Woolsey in Peach O'Reno
and specially selected supporting programme.
Musical divertissement on the Savoy Wonder Organ
by Mr. F.J. Bridgeman A.R.C.O.
Doors open at 7pm.
Only a limited number of seats. No advance booking.
Members of public bodies and prominent citizens
have kindly consented to be present.

The activities of the first night certainly didn't disappoint. Thousands of people congregated outside on Patrick Street, and the guards had their hands full trying to control the lively crowds. The events inside were a little more dignified. Lord Mayor Frank J. Daly performed the ceremony with the assistance of Richard Wallace, Chairman of Cork Harbour Commissioners. When the speeches ended, Fred Bridgeman made his debut on the stage of the Savoy and played the national anthem on the famous Compton organ. It was the beginning of a beloved Cork institution.

THE CITY HAD never before seen anything on the same scale as the Savoy. With its colourful art deco exterior and imposing lighted canopy, it was the most stylish and modern building on Patrick Street in the 1930s. The interior was equally elaborate and no expense was spared in any part of the building. A splendid staircase ran from the spacious marble foyer, through the restaurant, and into the Grand Circle where the most expensive seats in the house were located. To the rear of the Grand Circle lay the Gods which was the cheapest part of the house. There was a separate entrance to this section from William Street at the side, with a climb of 108 steps to the top. It was so high up it was known as 'Everest', and it was especially popular with schoolboys. The back stalls were the costliest section downstairs, while the front stalls provided more affordable accommodation.

Downstairs at the Savoy. Courtesy of Irish Examiner

The auditorium itself was modelled on a Venetian street and was a breathtaking sight to behold. The original programme described the interior as follows; "atmospheric decoration showing a wide panorama of boldly coloured walls, quaint windows, cypress tress climbing above old garden walls against blue skies, opulent grapes and trailing vines twining from old world rafters." A magnificent proscenium arch surrounded the stage and screen with ornamentation that was based on the Rialto Bridge in Venice, and plush draping tableau curtains featuring a picture of the Venetian Grand Canal covered the main centrepiece. The ceiling overhead was encrusted with small star-like lights that twinkled during the organ show, and one woman was so convinced she was looking at the real thing said, 'I hope it doesn't rain down on us'. For a period in the 1930s they also had a cloud machine to compliment the stars. That added the final idyllic touch to this most dazzling of picture palaces. In total the grand auditorium could hold 2,249 patrons, making it by far the largest cinema in Cork.

The grand stage and screen of the Savoy. Courtesy of Irish Examiner

TO GET WORK ANYWHERE in 1932 was quite an accomplishment, but to get a job in the Savoy was a great privilege. Providing a comfortable and hospitable service to the customers was the principal duty of the Savoy's workers, and a staff of seventy was carefully selected to perform this task. They worked under the guidance of a Rosscommon man named John McGrath who was the first resident manager of the cinema. All the employees were decked out in distinctive uniforms that set them apart from the rest of the working population, and it was often said that the ladies who worked there were so attractive and refined they could have competed in the Rose of Tralee. Among the most noted of the female staff were Gladys Leech who became one of Cork's most prominent artists, and Evelyn Weller who was the mother of musician Bob Geldof.

The spacious marble foyer of the Savoy. Courtesy of Irish Examiner

The head usher of the Savoy – or commisionaire as they were called back then – was John O'Connell from Blarney Street. Johnno, as he was best known, was a man familiar to thousands of Corkonians and his was the face that greeted the patrons as they arrived at the Savoy. He was a tall imposing figure who had fought in the British Army during World War I, although those who knew him recognised that he was a gentle giant. He brought many entertaining military tales back to Cork which he regularly told to amuse his colleagues. Among the most popular was a story about playing cards with the King of England. Like all employees of the Savoy, Johnno had the highest standards of presentation and cleanliness, and at the beginning of each working day he would examine the uniforms, shoes and hands of all the staff to make sure they met with his approval. No one ever appeared in damaged or dirty clothing, and a store of spare uniforms was kept under the stage to cover all eventualities. Organising the huge queues was also a part of his daily duties. Like a good soldier, he would manoeuvre the sometimes unruly crowds into single file before letting them inside. Occasionally someone at the back would cry out 'Rush!' to create a stampede, but they were rarely a match for Johnno who would stand firm and shout 'At your peril!' This always stopped everyone in their tracks.

THE STUDIOS OF Rank, United Artists, 20th Century Fox and Columbia supplied new films to the Savoy, and the programme changed twice a week on Sundays and Wednesdays. Over the years, the big pictures that played on their silver screen included *The Song of Bernadette, The Mark of Zorro, From Here To Eternity, On the Waterfront, The King and I,* and *Bridge on the River Kwai.* They were also the first cinema in Cork to introduce CinemaScope (wide-screen) with *The Robe* in September 1954. As well as presenting the big new movie of the week, the Savoy's programme always contained a good selection of supporting features including *Fitzpatrick's Travel Talk, Look at Life* and Irish Movie Tone News.

The newsreel by itself was a big attraction, as for many people it was the only means by which they could keep in touch with what was going on in the world. When a newsreel featured footage from a major sporting event such as the FA Cup or the Grand National, it would be specifically advertised in the papers and hundreds of people would go along to the cinema just to see that alone. If the news was more popular than the main film, it was often shown again after the feature for those who didn't get in to see it in time. Films were screened continuously in those days and a person could come in at his convenience and stay as long as he liked. People often arrived in half way through the picture. Usually they would watch the end of that show and wait for the part where they arrived to came around a second time before leaving. Because of the size of the Savoy it was easy for an eager fan to stay there all day, as the ushers had a difficult job trying to keep track of all the people and the different times they came in.

For the audience watching the pictures it seemed as if the running of the show was continuous, but behind the scenes there were many people at work in the operating box to keep things functioning smoothly. Every projection box employed four persons – three senior projectionists and one apprentice – and it was their job to keep the show on the road. The films came in individual reels of approximately twenty minutes in length and could only be shown one at a time. Because of this, each operating box had to have two projectors. When a reel was drawing to an end, a series of small circles would appear in the top right hand corner of the screen. That was the signal for the operator to switch power from the first projector to the second. During the show each operator had their own reel to look after, and they had to make sure that it ran on time and without interruption. When their reel was finished they could relax for twenty minutes or so until their next one came around. The Savoy's box was located right under the balcony, and it was hardly surprising that they had the biggest and best equipped operating box in town. They even had a third projector on standby in case either of the other two malfunctioned.

In October of 1946 the manager, Mr. Carroll, employed a young man named Dan Williamson as an assistant to the electrician Maurice Welsh. As the job was that of an assistant and not an apprentice, there wasn't much scope for promotion, so when a vacancy opened up in the operating box three months later, Dan started to learn the trade of showing films. Projection was a very skilled business in those days and when Dan began, it took up to five years training to become a full operator. During that period the apprentice had to learn all the different technical aspects of the craft, and in addition, they had to perform all the menial tasks for their seniors such as fetching the newspaper, or bringing them their tea. However, the apprentice's main job was to rewind the reels of film after they had ended, and it was for this reason that the young trainees were always known as 'rewind boys'. Over the years Dan rose up through the ranks to become the Savoy's chief operator, and he remained in that job until the cinema's final days.

IN THE ERA BEFORE television, Sunday was always 'the' night of the week to go to the pictures. Before returning to the hustle and bustle of work on a Monday morning, many thousands of people liked to engage in a bit of movie magic and the Savoy was always the number one place to go in Cork. To get tickets, people had to turn up on Wednesday with the stubs from the previous week to show that they were regulars. If they didn't, there was a waiting list containing the names of hundreds of others who were more than happy to take their place. Eamonn McSweeney from Donnybrook who was fortunate enough to have permanent seats at the Savoy said "Tickets were as scarce as hen's teeth." The demand for Sunday night was so great a black market developed which supplied tickets at inflated prices. The principal 'dealer' was a man from the Coal Quay called Paddy Kearney who, with his band of cronies, would call around to all the big cinemas earlier in the week and buy up as many seats as they could get. They would then sell them on to those who would otherwise be left out in the cold. He usually charged a 100% mark up on the tickets for the Savoy, and many fellows forked out the enormous costs if only to impress upon their girlfriends that money was no object.

Sunday night at the Savoy was such a special occasion that people would dress in their best clothes for the evening. In those days there were no matinees on a Sunday afternoon, so the anticipation for the big evening show was all the greater. Cinema queues were always large, none more so that the Savoy, and they always provided an ideal opportunity for local characters who were looking to make a few bob. One famous figure who always 'performed' for the crowds outside the Savoy was Jerry Bruton. By any standards he was a limited entertainer as his repertoire contained just one song called 'We'll all go down the Marina'. He would walk up and down the footpath singing his tune, and while he never begged or put out his hand, he would accept any gratuities that were offered to him.

The show itself would start with the first feature around 7.15 or 7.30pm. That was followed by an ice cream break when girls with trays of refreshments would walk around the cinema selling their wares. After that the Irish Movietone News was shown, then the organ show, a trailer, and finally the second feature. For many the main attraction of the night was the live musical performance of Fred Bridgeman, an organist who was the Savoy's top live entertainer for nearly thirty years. Born in Reading in 1896, Fred began his musical career as a chorister at Westminster Abbey when he was still just a boy. One of his most significant appearances in those choir stalls was for the coronation of King George V in 1910. He subsequently studied at the Trinity College of Music and worked as a private organist in England in the 1920s. Later he moved to Cork where he was employed in St. Lukes Church, but he achieved his lasting fame at the organ of the Savoy.

Fred Bridgeman's sing-a-long programmes were universally popular with all the patrons of the Savoy, and many people travelled up from Mallow and Fermoy just to hear him play. On Sunday nights he and his organ would arise from the bowels of the earth to the thunderous applause of the crowd. Each of his performances featured a good selection of modern and classical tunes, but 'The Legion of the Lost', the overture to 'William Tell' and 'Orpheus in the Underworld' were especially popular with his audience. Gladys Leech, the Savoy's artist in residence, illustrated

Fred Bridgeman enjoying a spot of fishing. Courtesy of Irish Examiner

the slides that accompanied the organ show. She would draw twenty or thirty slides per song, and the projectionists had to change these to keep in time with the music. At the conclusion of the performance, Bridgeman would take a single bow and then he and his organ would disappear from view under the stage. Such was the appeal of his shows that Radio Eireann began broadcasting them in 1952. His deputies George Rothwell, Norman Metcalfe and Gerard Shanahan performed the organist's duties in his absence, but they never managed to excite the crowd quite as effectively as he did. The Savoy was always a great venue for live performances, and music echoed throughout its hallowed halls all down through the years. Stars like Gracie Fields, Beniamino Gigli, Paul Robeson and Richard Tauber were among the big names who appeared on its stage, while in the 1960s it became a top venue for the new faces of rock and roll like Tom Jones, the Bee Gees and The Rolling Stones.

THE FILM FESTIVAL

THE CORK FILM INTERNATIONAL was born out of an annual spring festival called An Tostal, which was started in 1953. This yearly event was a celebration of music, culture and the arts, and one of its principal organisers, a Waterford man named Dermot Breen, recognised the potential for a Cork festival devoted

exclusively to the celebration of films. With the assistance of Bord Failte, the first Cork Film International was staged in May 1956, and as the Savoy was the largest and best equipped cinema in the city, it was chosen to host this prestigious event. The opening film on May 21st was *A Town Called Alice,* and the stars of the film Peter Finch and Maureen Swanson along with actors John Gregson, Tony Wright, Josephine Griffin and June

Dermot Breen

Thorburn came to Cork to promote the event. President Sean T O'Kelly officiated at inaugural festival, and a brass band was present to play him in on the first night.

Under Dermot Breen's skilled guidance, the Cork Film International became one of the most prestigious festivals in the world. At its peak in the 1950s and 1960s, the Film Festival attracted crowds of up to 32,000 people annually, and the tickets for the event would sell out within days of the advertisements appearing in the paper. It provided a forum for the distinguished film fan to see high quality pictures from around the globe, and it offered a week of unparalleled excitement and glamour for the ordinary people of Cork. In the hours before the evening show, thousands of people would converge on Patrick Street to get a good spot to see the stars. The exterior of the cinema was decorated with all the flags from the participating countries, and a big spotlight was brought in to highlight the famous faces as they emerged from the hired cars and taxis. It was like Hollywood in Cork.

Crowds on Patrick Street for the first Film Festival in 1956. Courtesy of Irish Examiner

The parade of stars coming to town got longer each year as word of the hospitality and friendliness of Cork spread around the film world. Dame Flora Robson, Anna Neagle, Herbert Wilcox, Boris Karloff, Peter Cushing and James Mason were just a few of the big names to participate in the event, while the Irish actor Noel Purcell always attended for the craic. Each night before the main feature, one of the guests would be interviewed on the stage of the Savoy. After the show, all the participants would return to the festival club in the City Hall for an evening of music, dancing and merriment. Seasoned moviegoer Pat Mulcahy remembers the festival club as a place where the stars would gather and mix with the ordinary people of Cork. He recalls talking to actors Kenneth More, Carroll Baker and Virginia Mayo without any of the security restrictions that exist today. He said "You could sit down and talk to them".

The Glamour of the Film Festival in the early years. Noel Purcell can be seen in the background. Courtesy of Irish Examiner

The presence of famous screen actors on the streets of Cork gave people an opportunity to see stars as they were in real life. Actor Trevor Howard was a regular visitor to the city for many years, and nothing delighted him more than going to the pubs along the quays and drinking with the dockers. However, not all were quite so modest. Dawn Addams, the English actress, was a guest of the festival in the early 1960s. According to legend, she famously asked for a milk bath when staying at the Metropole Hotel. Pasteurised milk had just come on the market, and she was asked if she wanted the milk for the bath to be pasteurised (past your eyes). 'No,' she said, 'just up to my ass will be fine'.

FOR ONE WEEK each year the Savoy was home to the festival, and their hard working staff had to put in an extra effort to stage the greatest show in town. Carl McEnri was the manager at the time of the first festival, and he was responsible for co-ordinating all the activities within the cinema. Andy Condon, the Savoy's head maintenance man, was always kept especially busy throughout that week and one of his most important tasks was operating the spotlight that illuminated all the celebrities as they arrived. The opening day of the first festival in 1956 had special significance for him as it was the day his fourth child was born. Many of the visiting dignitaries stopped to enquire after his wife and child.

The projectionists were often the unsung heroes of the Film Festival, and they had to contend not just with the pressure of showing the films, but projecting them the way their makers intended. The director, Otto Preminger, was in town one year for the screening of his film *St Joan,* which was one of the first films to feature the new Saul Bass titles. An old man named Jack Brosnan was the operator in charge for the preview screening of Preminger's film. As he was not familiar with the new titles, Mr. Brosnan moved the film up and down in order to centre the titles in the middle of the screen – despite the fact that they were supposed to be positioned in the corners and not in the middle. A few seconds after he did this, there was a thumping noise in the corridor outside and Preminger stormed into the projection room. In a thick German accent he bellowed to Brosnan 'What are you doing to my film? What are you doing to my picture? Those are Saul Bass titles and they must be left exactly where they are!' Not really knowing who Preminger was, Mr. Brosnan turned around and said 'Don't worry, it'll be all right tonight Mr. Dillinger.'

While the format of the Festival may have changed considerably over the years, its spirit still remains the same to this day. Gone is the glamour and sophistication, the tuxedos and evening dresses, along with the eccentric behaviour of the visiting stars. It may no longer capture the attention of the whole city the way it did in the 1950s and 1960s, but each year it still draws thousands of people to the fine displays of international cinema that are on offer. Now as it approaches its 50th Anniversary, the Festival remains an important forum for filmmakers, fans and buffs to come together to share their common interest.

*   *   *

DESPITE THE ARRIVAL of Irish television in 1962, the immediate affects did not impact on the big cinemas. The Savoy was initially sheltered from the new technology as they were fortunate to show many of the great films of that decade including *Lawrence of Arabia, To Kill a Mocking Bird, Airport, The Graduate* and *The Great Escape.* The thrilling heroics of James Bond first hit the big screen in 1962 with *Dr. No,* and each instalment drew larger numbers than the last. New box office records were set when *Goldfinger* was shown in the Savoy in October of 1964, yet when the Disney fable *Mary Poppins* opened there in August of 1965, over fifty thousand people went to see it in its first two weeks alone. That was about half the population of the city!

Sadly bad times followed good, and as 1970 approached the character of the Savoy was starting to fade. Fred Bridgeman retired in 1967, having served the people of Cork since the cinema's opening in 1932. His departure signalled the end of the era of the cinema organ and the grand sing-a-long shows that kept so many people entertained. On retiring, the manager Jimmy Campbell described him as a first rate musician, a sentiment that was echoed by everyone who ever heard him play. Three years later, Mr. Russell Wynn from Kilbrittain Castle in West Cork bought the organ and installed it in his home. It was so big and contained such an elaborate system of pipes, it took two weeks to dismantle and would take more than a year to reassemble.

From 1962 to 1972, annual attendance's at the Savoy had fallen from 1,000,000 per annum to just 200,000. In an effort to make things more economically viable, the capacity of the cinema was reduced by 300 in order to provide more space for patrons, and certain parts of the auditorium were closed except for very busy nights. Unfortunately, they were becoming few and far between. The calibre of the films on show declined rapidly, and consequently so did the crowds. It was not uncommon for just twenty or thirty people to attend a matinee performance, and with figures like that the cinema just couldn't stay in business. In July of 1973, the

Savoy's parent company announced with regret that the closure was nigh. Despite efforts to get a stay of execution, the projectors rolled for the last time eighteen months later.

For the Savoy's staff of sixty, the closure had a major impact on their lives as many had devoted much of their careers to that cinema. Andy Condon the head maintenance man, worked there for 39 years, operators Dan Williamson and Derry Seymour

Former Savoy employees, Dan Williamson and Andy Condon

28 years and 21 years respectively, while chief cleaner Michael O'Brien had been a part of that cinema since 1933. The final manager was Mrs. Renee Ahern, who joined the ranks as a secretary and worked her way up to the top position in 1973. She was the first woman to hold that job. For them it had been a happy environment in which to work, and a place where lasting friendships were made. The closure was an equally sad occasion for the people of Cork as the Savoy had been the gold standard in comfort, elegance, luxury, good films and hospitable service. As Dan Williamson put it, "The Savoy was a cinema – all the others were picture houses." We may never see its like again.

THE PAVILION

AMIDST THE TERROR AND confusion of the War of Independence, the Pavilion Cinema and Restaurant Ltd at 80, 81 Patrick Street opened on Thursday March 10th, 1921. It was a time when the city was ruled by Martial Law, and because of the escalating violence and social unrest, the British authorities imposed a severe curfew on all citizens of Cork which compelled

The Pavilion in the 1930s. Courtesy of Irish Examiner

them to be indoors by tea time. Under these difficult circumstances, the Pavilion opened its doors with a single presentation of D.W. Griffith's epic *The Greatest Question*. The Pav drew a capacity crowd on its first day, many of whom were curious to see the inside of the new Patrick Street landmark. During its building period, thousands of passers by had stopped to view the imposing and spacious entrance and the grand limestone façade. When it opened for business, the interiors proved to be as impressive as the outside. A majestic flight of broad marble stairs ascended from the centre of the hallway to the café and ballroom upstairs, and the plush 900 seater auditorium was fitted with comfortable cushioned seats that were provided by the famous Cork department store the Munster Arcade.

The Tallon family from the Rochestown Road were the owners of this new cinema, and Fred Harford was the first manager. He brought much experience to the job as he previously worked in the Abbey Theatre as an actor and in latter times as manager. Kevin O'Donovan was the cinema's chief projectionist and electrician, and Tim Kelly from Kerry was the first commisionaire. Mr. Kelly had come to Cork looking for work and was employed on the construction of the cinema. After his work on the building was complete, the foreman recommended him to Mr. Tallon for the job as head usher due to his amenable personality. His employment heralded the beginning of the Kelly family's dynasty in the Pavilion. His daughter Margaret (Peggy) worked there for nearly forty years as did his son Donal, who would rise up through the ranks to become the manager in the 1980s.

The Pavilion quickly established itself as the finest cinema in the city. Few picture houses offered the extensive orchestral music that the Pav provided to accompany the silent films, but when the sound revolution arrived they were the first to respond. For a number of weeks in July and August of 1929, the Pavilion cancelled all afternoon matinees so that the engineers from Western Electric could install the sound system. The talkies made their debut on Monday the 5th of August with an Al Jolson film *The Singing Fool*. It caused a huge stir in Cork and drew in 12,000 people in the first five days alone. To cater for the demand, the management added an extra show each day at 12.30pm for the convenience of patrons travelling from the country.

Although talking films were here to stay, many people were sceptical about the new medium and with good reason. The soundtracks were scratchy and often inaudible, and many Irish people found the American accent difficult to understand. Just four months after the arrival of sound, the management of the Pavilion had to go out of their way to reassure many wary customers that talking pictures would not spoil their film going experiences. In January of 1930 they showed *Bulldog Drummond,* a story about an ex-British army officer who yearned for adventure, played by Ronald Coleman in his first speaking part. The Pav took out large ads in the local papers to convince the public that the experience of talking pictures was a positive one. The move worked, and *Bulldog Drummond* became a tremendous success.

While pictures were the Pavilion's main source of entertainment in its first decade of life, the auditorium also had a stage on which live shows, recitals and concerts were frequently held to great popular acclaim. However on the morning of February 16th 1930, disaster struck when a fire swept through the building. A passing guard sounded the alarm and alerted the fire brigade. The manager, Mr. Ernest Wates, along with the dedicated staff assisted the fire fighters with their efforts, but when the flames were finally extinguished the damage could then be seen. The stage, screen and 'talkie' loud speakers were destroyed, as were the front row of seats and much of the ornate plaster work on the walls and ceiling. Such was the heat generated from the fire that the timber work in the distant balcony was scorched. Fortunately, a real inferno was averted when steel boxes of films were rescued just before they combusted. Nonetheless the Pavilion was severely gutted. It reopened, fully remodelled and redecorated the following June. The newly constructed Pavilion once again set the standards by which all the others would be judged, although the stage was not rebuilt and sadly no more live performers would ever grace that venue.

FOR MORE THAN HALF a century, the restaurant in the Pavilion was one of the most fashionable places to dine in Cork. The room in which it was housed was lavishly carpeted with an open fireplace at either end, and it offered its customers a wonderful view of Patrick Street. From the 1920s to the 1950s, it was managed by Miss Murphy, with her niece Nora White, the assistant manager. In an era when customers had high expectations, this restaurant provided a top class service. Every table had a white cloth and fresh flowers, and if anything was spilled the cloth was taken away immediately and replaced. The silver and the crockery were polished every night.

Michael McCarthy went to work in the Pavilion as a pageboy in 1939, and eventually became one of the senior members of the ushering staff. He witnessed the running of the restaurant first hand and recalls its heyday in great detail. In 1939, 1s 6d bought a four course meal that consisted of soup and a bun made by Thompsons, a main course (roast beef, potatoes, vegetables), a sweet, and tea or coffee. All the food was locally supplied and was of the highest quality. Mr. Wates, the manager of the cinema, introduced coloured menus and he also named some of the meals after places in Cork such as Mardyke Tea, Marina Tea, and Lads of the Village. The restaurant was always a very exclusive place, and many of the Cork 'Aristocracy' who held parliament there included Mr. Thornhill the solicitor, Sir Stanley Harrington, and Mr. Woodward the Auctioneer. Micheal MacLiammoir, the famous stage actor, was another regular customer when he was in town. He would walk up the stairs with a coat draped over his shoulders and make a grand entrance, with his colleague Hilton Edwards just behind. Eamon de Valera occasionally stopped by on his trips to Cork.

The city's local characters also paid frequent visits to the Pav and its restaurant down through the years. The traders from Cornmarket Street were among the most colourful and shrewd business people in Cork back then, and Tim Kelly the Pav's commisionaire, often engaged in commercial transactions with them. Mr. Kelly saved the cracked ware from the café and sold it to the dealers on the Coal Quay. They in turn traded it to large families who were constantly looking for bits of crockery to replace the pieces that got broken. At Christmas time, Mr. Kelly bargained with them again to buy the holly and ivy to adorn the restaurant. He haggled with them on the street to get the best price possible, but when the deal was done they all went into the Roundy House on the corner of the Coal Quay for a couple of drinks.

THE CORK CINEMA COMMUNITY suffered a terrible tragedy in late 1947 when Tim Kelly was killed in a traffic accident on the Western Road. It was a huge shock to everyone in the business as he had been a very prominent and popular figure among the employees of Cork's cinemas. When his funeral procession passed through town, all of the picture houses turned off their lights as a mark of respect to their colleague. A month after his death, his son Donal left school and went to work in the Pavilion in his father's place. He would stay there for the next forty two years until it

Pat Mulcahy and former Pavilion manager Donal Kelly

closed in 1989, after which he was transferred to the new Capitol Cineplex as manager. He was the third member of his family to come to work in the Pav, as his sister Peggy had started working there as an usherette several years earlier.

For his new job, Donal was decked out in a uniform which consisted of a navy jacket and cap, and a white shirt, similar in style to that of the Bengal Lancers, . Kevin O'Donovan was the manager when Donal began, having been promoted from chief operator some years earlier. His brother was the actor Harry O'Donovan, who was also a scriptwriter for Jimmy O'Dea. Mr. O'Donovan was a very good and well liked manager, and he loved to spend the

Pavilion manager Kevin O'Donovan, taken at the projector in the 1920s.
Courtesy of Philip O'Donovan

evening in the foyer greeting the customers as they arrived. He had very high standards of etiquette befitting a man in his position, and he ensured that the staff were always on their best behaviour when the cinema was open. However the patrons often had a soft spot for the workers, and as Donal Kelly recalls, "The people who would come in on Sunday nights would be the prominent people, and they'd always stuff a few sweets into your pocket."

Because it was such an ornate cinema with a very elegant restaurant, the Pavilion was always a suitable place to take a date. The couples had their permanent seats for the Sunday night shows, and Donal Kelly got to know many of them personally. "The people you would meet in the cinemas that time – they were lovely people." When he was about eighteen he took his first trip to Dublin, and while there he met one of the Pav's regular couples who were on their honeymoon. The films on offer always pleased the romantics in the crowd too. The Pav had a contract to show all

Crowds at a midnight screening of Showboat at the Pav, taken in the early 1950s. Courtesy of Irish Examiner

the MGM films, which were among the finest Hollywood extravaganzas of the golden age of movie making. MGM produced many of the films of Clark Gable, Spencer Tracy, Gene Kelly, Mickey Rooney and Judy Garland, and were responsible for some of the greatest hits of the day including *Show Boat, Singin' in the Rain,* the *Lassie* films and the *Andy Hardy* series. Musicals were their speciality and when a particularly big film was on show, the queues stretched all the way down Patrick Street and sometimes reached the door of St. Peter and Paul's church.

The most beloved stars to grace the screen of the Pavilion in that era were romantic musical team of Jeanette MacDonald and Nelson Eddy. Jeanette MacDonald was adept at playing light comedy, but she also had a fine soprano voice which made her suitable for a wide variety of films. Nelson Eddy was an accomplished singer with a background in opera who became a big star when he was teamed opposite Jeanette MacDonald in a number of romantic operettas. Their first film together was *Naughty Marietta* in which she played a French princess who runs off to America. There she falls in love with an Indian scout played by Nelson Eddy. In total they made eight films together including *Rose Marie, The Girl of the Golden West, Sweethearts* and *May Time.* The stories in many of their films varied little, and they both tended to play similar characters, but every time their films were shown in the Pav they always managed to pack the house. An average film ran for a week in the Pavilion, but when Nelson Eddie & Jeanette MacDonald were in town their films were usually retained for a second week.

Hollywood's highest creation is arguably *Gone With the Wind,* David O. Selznick's epic production of Margaret Mitchell's best-selling novel about the American Civil War. Made in 1939, it starred the then 'King of Hollywood' Clark Gable as Rhett Butler and the unknown Vivien Leigh as the feisty Scarlett O'Hara. Featuring romance, war, heartbreak, death, destruction, resurrection and one word of obscene language that caused quite a calamity on its original release, it was the most sensational picture ever produced. *Gone With The Wind* first came to Cork during the war years when it was shown at the Savoy, yet over the next quarter of a century it made many repeat visits and it was always to the Pavilion it came. To tie in with the film's immense appeal, the restaurant always served a special *Gone With The Wind* tea during the intermission. Donal Kelly developed a immense knowledge about films in his many years working in the business, and reckons that nothing has come along in the sixty years since *Gone With The Wind* that has surpassed it.

KEVIN O'DONOVAN, the distinguished manager of the Pavilion died in 1954, and the current owner Mrs Murphy had considerable difficulty finding a suitable replacement for him. Leo Ward was an independent film distributor from Dublin who came to Cork regularly on business and frequently booked films into the Pavilion. Mrs Murphy offered him the job as manager because of his considerable experience, and although initially reluctant to accept, he eventually decided to oversee it on a part time basis. While he had his own film distribution business to operate, he agreed to come to Cork every month to attend to the running of the Pavilion. He refused to accept the generous salary which Mrs Murphy offered him, and instead agreed to do the job for half. However, in the first year he managed to book in pictures that pulled in big crowds and so he was rewarded with the other half as a bonus.

Mr. Ward's career in the film business began in 1939 when he started working for an independent film distributor in his native city of Dublin. After three months his life changed dramatically when he was signed by Manchester City Football Club. Unfortunately the outbreak of World War II interrupted his football career, so he returned to Dublin to resume his job in the cinema industry. He continued playing soccer during the war, this time with Drumcondra, and he made many visits to Cork to play on the Mardyke. He set up his own film distribution company in 1948 with his step brother Kevin Anderson, and this also brought him to Cork regularly. He developed a fondness for the city and forged some strong ties with the contacts he made in the cinemas. His success as manager of the Pavilion, and his reputation as a very capable business man, resulted in his company being offered an option to buy the Lee Cinema when the holders decided to sell in the late 1950s.

Ward and Anderson bought up many picture houses in the late 1950s and early 1960s, and they kept them in business when the industry hit hard times. Mrs Murphy later sold them a half interest in the Pavilion, and within a decade, they purchased the

Abbey Films directors Kevin Anderson and Leo Ward, taken in the 1960s. Courtesy of Leo Ward

premises outright. They appointed the book keeper Miss Josephine Kelleher as manager, and she stayed in charge for many years. Like all her predecessors, she ran the premises as if it was her own and took immense pride in its maintenance. In the 1950s and 1960s, the Pav continued to enjoy big financial successes with the British comedy *Carry On* series, and distinguished dramas like *War and Peace, Ice Cold in Alex* and *Dr. Zhivago* also drew full houses. However, when the Bruce Lee film *Enter The Dragon* played there in the early 1970s, it attracted a crowd of quite rowdy individuals. After its first night, there was blood on the marble steps outside from people imitating what they had seen in the picture.

While RTE's first broadcast dealt an inevitable blow to the cinema industry, the Pavilion generally remained one of the more sophisticated places in town. The restaurant was often used for workshops during the Film Festival, and such noted personalities as Francois Truffaut, Trevor Howard, Edgar Bergin, Patrick Wayne (son of John) and Jane Seymour stopped by to give classes for film students. Many of the celebrities paused to have a few words with the staff as well. However, in the late 1960s, a genuine piece of film history occurred at the Pav when the legendary director David Lean came to town. Donal Kelly was on hand to witness this momentous event: "When David Lean came here [to Ireland] to make *Ryan's Daughter* he had George C. Scott in mind for the role eventually played by Robert Mitchum. They arranged to send three reels from three films featuring George C. Scott down from Dublin. David Lean was touring around Kerry at the time looking for a spot to make the film, and they decided that Cork would be the handiest place for him to view the reels." He and his secretary arranged a morning time to watch the reels of film in the Pavilion, and it was Donal that the manageress asked to go up and stay with them in the balcony. "I had the balcony to myself with David Lean and his lady secretary and a couple of other lads. When it was over they gave me a fiver which was good money at the time."

EPIC DRAMAS LIKE *Gandhi, Amadeus, Fatal Attraction* and *Out of Africa* brought crowds to the Pav in the 1980s the likes of which had not been seen in years, but it was the magical *E.T. The Extra Terrestrial* that became one of the biggest success stories in the cinema's history. In that decade Donal Kelly ascended to the role of manager following the retirement of Miss Kelleher, and in the Pavilion's last few years he preserved the high standards that had been its trademark since the 1920s. Sadly, spiralling costs led to the closure of the famous restaurant in 1985. For over sixty years this glorious emporium had attracted thousands of different visitors from all walks of life. However by the 1980s, a plethora of new modern restaurants and cafés existed in all parts of the city, and the Pav's restaurant was no longer viable. The cinema's days were numbered too. Despite its irreplaceable Old World charm, the owners had plans for the future of Cork's cinemas that no longer included the Pavilion. It closed in August of 1989 with a screening of *Indiana Jones and the Last Crusade* as its final film. After that, going to the pictures in Cork would never be the same again.

THE PALACE
The House with the Perfect Sound

DAN LOWREY WAS the last great man of show business in the 19th Century. Single-handedly he transformed the face of Irish theatre, laid the foundation stones for the arrival of cinema, and created a legacy that still continues today. The son of an Irish emigrant from Roscrea, he was born Thomas Lowrey in Leeds in 1841. From an early age he learned the business of entertainment from his father Dan Sr., who had achieved much success as a professional performer in the first half of the 19th Century. Later in life Dan Sr. built up an empire of taverns and theatres in England, which provided top of the range music hall entertainment of its time. He returned to Ireland in the 1870s to expand his enterprises in his native country, and in 1878 he opened the Star of Erin

The Palace on MacCurtain Street

Music Hall on Dame Street in Dublin. When his health deteriorated in the following decade, his son took over the Irish side of the business. In keeping with tradition he changed his name from Thomas to Dan, and he competed with the London syndicates to attract the biggest names to the Star of Erin. In April of 1896 that venue screened the first ever moving picture show in Ireland.

By the mid 1890's, Dan Jr. realised that there was enormous potential for entertainment in Ireland and so he decided to expand to Cork. Local magistrates granted him a licence to build the Palace of Varieties, and King Street (now MacCurtain Street) was decided upon as the location for his new music hall. The new theatre, which could accommodate 1500 patrons, was luxuriously fitted with the best seats and carpets, and the lighting was powered by electricity. Garnishing its entrance was a magnificent canopy which survived well into the 20th Century, until a speeding motorist collided with it one day. Dan Lowrey, who was present on the first night on

The magnificent proscenium arch of the Palace's stage

Easter Monday 1897, pledged to spare no expense in securing the best talent on offer in the world of show business. The opening programme featured a number of live acts along with "Professor Jolly's World Renowned Cinematographe" – a series of animated and moving pictures. One of them showed the arrival of the Russian Czar and Czarina into Paris. Prices ranged from £1 for the private boxes on the stage, down to 6d for a seat in the balcony. The

The opulent auditorium of the Palace

reaction of Cork people to the Palace was as favourable as Dan expected, and shortly afterwards he opened a third music hall 'The Alhambra' in Belfast. Sadly, the strain of managing the different venues started to affect his health, and he died in August of 1898.

Despite the death of the great visionary, the Palace of Varieties became one of the best entertainment facilities in Cork in the new century. Top vaudevillian names from Ireland and England regularly performed on its stage, yet from the early 1900s, its programme always contained a series of short films in a presentation known as 'the Palascope'. This proved to be a great novelty with their audience. The exhibition of films in those times was extremely costly, and advertisements for the Palace often emphasised the expense that was incurred when a film was shown. However the Palascope's popularity increased over time, and with the cinema business booming in the city by the 1920s, the Palace started screening film seasons annually.

Under the direction of the manager Richard McGrath, the Palace permanently became a picture house in June of 1930. It was the time when talkies were arriving on the scene, and the newly equipped Palace labelled themselves 'The House With The Perfect Sound'. One of their main successes in the early years was Charlie Chaplin's masterpiece *City Lights* which opened in November 1931. At a time when cinemas changed their films at least once if not twice a week, *City Lights* ran for a long period of time, with over 10,000 people going to see it in its first week alone. Chaplin started his career as a vaudevillian performer on the London stage, and in the early 1900s he was one of many top acts to play live on the stage of the Palace in Cork. He was in many respects a prophetic figure in show business as he was one of the many entertainers lured away from the live stage to the big screen. As the music hall tradition was ultimately replaced by cinema, it was fitting that Chaplin's movie creations should return to great applause years later. However it was ironic that a silent film like *City Lights* was such a hit in 'The House with the Perfect Sound'.

SOMETIMES CHANCE ENCOUNTERS can change lives, and when a young man named Michael Murphy and his sister Rosie met Michael Dineen in town one day in 1933, his life was transformed in the blink of an eye. Mr. Dineen was then the chief projectionist in the Palace, and he offered the eighteen year old Michael a job as an apprentice operator. Michael promptly accepted and would remain at the Palace for the next fifty years. The early 1930s saw widespread unemployment in Ireland as a result of the economic war with England, so during Michael's early years in the job he had to work especially long and hard hours to make his money. In those days he earned the modest salary of 7s 6d a week, and on average he would have to work sixty or seventy hours with just one day off. As he didn't get any breaks to go home for his dinner, his sister would have to bring his sandwiches down to MacCurtain Street.

Like the apprentices in the other cinemas, Michael had to undertake many of the smaller and more difficult jobs, and one of his many duties was to collect the reels of film from Kent Station on a Sunday afternoon. Because the Palace was known as 'the House with the Perfect Sound', the despatch workers at the station nicknamed Michael 'the Sound Man'. In the 1930s, the Palace shared the same Pathe News reel with the Lee Cinema. Michael

Mr. Michael Murphy

would often have to rush down to Winthrop Street with the film under his arm after they had finished with it on MacCurtain Street. In later years, the Palace showed British Movie Tone News and these reels frequently contained footage of the Royal Family. At a time when republican sentiments were running high, such material was very unpopular in some circles, so Michael had to get a Garda escort from the station to the cinema in case members of the IRA tried to seize the film from him.

Michael's boss, the chief operator Mr. Dineen, was a very strict task master who enforced a strong code of rules in the operating box. Because the reels of films were so highly flammable, he would search all those who came into the projection room for matches lest the films would go up in smoke. Michael was responsible for showing thousands of films in his fifty year career, but fortunately none of them ever caught fire. The first he had a hand in projecting was a British musical called *The Waltz* starring

Evelyn Laye, and among the most popular actors that appeared on the screen of the Palace in his early years were Ralph Lynn, Robertson Hare, Gracie Fields, Conrad Veidt, Jesse Mathews and Jan Kippura. The teenage singing sensation Deanna Durbin was one of the biggest stars of the 1930s and 1940s, and her films *Mad About Music, That Certain Age* and *It Started With Eve* received their first Cork runs at the Palace. Because she had a near universal appeal, Miss Durbin's pictures would always draw crowds big enough to sell out the house. While many of her fans were women, all the 'tough boys' queued up to see her films too.

HAVING CHANGED OWNERS on several occasions since Dan Lowrey's time in charge, the grand MacCurtain Street cinema

Mr. Bill Aherne

became the property of the Daly family from Blackrock. They were prominent local business people whose commercial interests also included Sutton's Coal. A gentleman named Bill Aherne took over from Richard McGrath as manager in the mid 1930s, and he had a large staff under his command. The head usher was a man named Neilus Farrell from Grattan Street, who was known as 'Dorian Grey' to his fellow workers. He had a very flamboyant personality, and he often welcomed members of the staff in the morning with a roar of 'Greetings and Salutations, and if you belong to the hunt – Tally Ho!'

The brothers Dan and Neilus Cronin were also senior members of the ushering staff. Dan in particular was a very fussy man as far as queuing was concerned, and he was very strict with the crowds of people who gathered on MacCurtain Street to get into the 4d rush upstairs. Like the 4d section in every cinema, it was the preferred division with schoolboys and others who were short of the few pence needed to sit in the more comfortable seats downstairs. Because of his precision, he was nicknamed 'tidy me nice' by the women with shawls. To annoy him they'd call out 'Here comes 'tidy me nice'. If we had a hat on us we wouldn't be shoved around like this. It's only because we have a shawl.' The Balcony consisted of long wooden benches and had a capacity for 450 persons, but no one could pack in more people than Dan Cronin. It was reputed to be the roughest spot in the house, and one time somebody threw a dead cat over the side.

Miss Mulcahy from the Lower Road was one of the ticket sellers, and she had been a part of the staff since the theatre's variety days. She was a constant presence watching all the crowds coming and going, and she became acquainted with many of the customers personally. A young Donal Kelly was one person she knew from his regular trips to the cinema. Because his father was the head usher in the Pavilion, he was given special treatment in many of the other picture houses and the Palace was one of his favourites. He recalls "We'd all go down to the Palace on a Saturday, and we'd be warned by my mother to get the sour milk for the baking on the way and we were given a gallon container. We were also sent down to St. Patrick's for confession." One day he and his friends went down to see a Robin Hood film with the gallon of sour milk, which they brought right into the auditorium and left under the seat during the show. As audiences tended to be lively and buoyant, someone sitting behind kicked over the can sending the milk flowing all around the cinema. They all went outside looking for mops to clean it up and thought they would be thrown out permanently. "We thought we would never be left back in there again, and we were also afraid to go home as we didn't have the sour milk or money to buy any more. However, Miss Mulcahy went into the cloakroom and came back with some money to replace the milk which she stored for us while we watched the rest of the film."

DERMOT BREEN CAME to the Palace as manager in 1956 following the death of Bill Aherne. Mr. Breen was a prominent person in the film community as he was the director of the Cork Film Festival, and later he became the Irish Film Censor. Following the burning of the Opera House in Christmas 1955, there was a notable absence of live theatre in Cork, so Mr. Breen filled the gap by bringing live shows back to the stage of the Palace. Although they were required to put on two performances a year to retain their bar licence, the Palace had long since neglected its theatrical side. Yet under Mr. Breen's direction it flourished again. Among the big names to act on the Palace's fine stage over the next few years were Jack Cruise, Danny Cummins, Micheal MacLiammoir, Cyril Cusack, James N. Healy, Maureen Potter and Jimmy O'Dea. Maureen Potter once claimed that the stage of the Palace was one of the best on which she ever performed. During that time the Cork Grand Opera Group made the Palace their new home, and staged several major productions there including *La Traviata, Rigoletto* and *Faust*. The projectionists who would otherwise have been idle during the theatrical seasons, worked the lighting and filled in as stage hands.

Shortly after he arrived, Mr. Breen also made several significant changes to the running of the cinema. He made the Palace's performance continuous for the first time in its history, and an extra operator was hired to work the new 5-7 shift. This job was given to Barry Leahy from Red Abbey Street, who had previously been a projectionist in the Assembly Rooms and the Lee. Pre-empting the threats that television would pose to the business, Mr. Breen initiated a series of alterations to the auditorium in 1959. The size of the cinema was reduced from 1000 to 600 seats, and the famous wooden benches in the gods were removed and replaced with individual soft bottomed seating. The contentment of the patrons was considered especially important, and the Palace willingly sacrificed seating space to ensure film goers would have more leg room. The new Palace was reopened in December 1959 by Minister Jack Lynch, who was also one of their regular customers.

Despite the many transformations and upheavals the cinema experienced in the 1950s, the Palace had one stroke of very good luck in that decade when they received the valuable contract to show pictures from the studio of MGM. This gave them access to such musical delights as *Lili* and *Gigi*, and Alfred Hitchcock's thriller *North by Northwest*. However, their biggest hit of all was the epic *Ben Hur*. This film ran for over nine weeks in the autumn of 1961 and was seen by over 60,000 people. At an early screening of *Ben Hur* at the Palace, someone spotted a motor car in the background during the chariot race. Mr. Breen subsequently pointed it out to the MGM personnel on one of his trips to Hollywood, and their explanation was that one of the reels had not been retrieved in time. If the film didn't provide enough drama, there was a severe thunder and lightening storm one day which interfered with the electricity supply to the projector. Michael Murphy and Barry Leahy were on duty in the box that evening, and they had to work frantically throughout the show to keep the film from breaking down. All night long the picture was going on and off, but when it came to the chariot race there was a calm in the storm and they were able to show that exciting scene without interference. However the moment the race was over, the lightening flashed again and the picture blacked out. To the annoyance of the operators and audience alike, it continued like that for the rest of the night.

FOLLOWING THE CLOSURE of the Savoy in the 1970s, the Palace became one of the temporary homes to the Cork Film Festival. A number of famous faces and names from the world of show business visited the theatre, including the British director Alan Parker who was present to promote his film *Midnight Express*. Sean Connery was in town the same year as he was making *The Great Train Robbery* in Kent Station. He too called to the Palace, although he didn't appear on stage with the other guests. Michael Murphy, who had been promoted to chief operator in 1975, met with all the dignitaries and said Alan Parker was a very modest person to talk to. Michael controlled the reigns of the Palace's operating box until he retired in May of 1984, having served the cinema for more than half a century. Such was his dedication to his job that he missed only two days of work in his first forty six years. Barry Leahy, who had himself worked there for a quarter of a century, stepped up to take his place.

By the time Michael retired, ticket sales had been severely hit by competition from television and videos. Good films like *Superman* and *Chariots of Fire* did well, but good films were becoming increasingly rare. One afternoon, a single old age pensioner was the only customer in attendance, yet the show had to go ahead. The writing was on the wall and on the June bank holiday weekend in 1988, the Palace showed its last ever film. However, this grand old theatre would rise from the ashes again. It was purchased by the Everyman Theatre Company, and in 1990 it reopened as a venue for live shows. In 1997, for the 100th anniversary, its interiors were fully refurbished and a new bar was installed. Outside, a grand canopy was erected over the main entrance. Every effort was made to restore the building to its original style, so that for the 21st Century Dan Lowrey's vision can continue to burn as brightly as it did in the past.

THE CAPITOL
Quality Pictures and Courteous Service

DURING THE EASTER WEEKEND in 1947, the Palace celebrated its half centenary in business with a rendition of Old Tyme Music Hall. Sadly few people came along to see the show, and one of the performers, Derry Fagan, commented that 'everyone must be down at the opening of the new cinema.' That new cinema was the ultra modern and spacious Capitol Cinema on the Grand Parade. Grants Shoe Shop burnt down in April of 1942, leaving a huge gap in one of the city's main commercial districts. Capitol and Allied Cinemas purchased the premises and built a new theatre on the site which opened on April 5th, 1947. It was the first new cinema in Cork since the Ritz joined the scene in 1939, and it was the second largest in the city holding over 1,300 patrons. The

The Capitol Cinema in days gone by. Courtesy of Irish Examiner

49

opening ceremony was performed by Canon O'Keeffe of the North Cathedral, in the presence of many dignitaries from Capitol and Allied Cinemas, and there was a strong feeling among all those present that the new cinema would live up to the company's motto 'quality pictures and courteous service'.

As far as quality pictures went, the programme for the opening night didn't disappoint. The main film was the Bob Hope and Joan Caulfield comedy *Monsieur Beaucaire,* and the supporting features included a Popeye cartoon *She Sick Sailors,* a documentary about flour milling called *Grist of the Mill,* and a Little Lulu cartoon *I'm Just Curious* which was presented in Technicolor. Ticket prices ranged from 1s to 2s 6d, but those who paid the admission were amazed by what they got in return. Seamus Quinn went to the Capitol shortly after it opened. Growing up he had been well acquainted with picture houses and would pursue a long career in the business himself, but he was quite taken aback by this new cinema in 1947. "There was the new smell off it – everything was new! The seats were new, the carpets were new, the paint was new, the building was new, and everything looked so different. Everything looked so stale in the other cinemas and so fresh in the Capitol."

Photo stills of films and stars lined the walls of the stairs, and a lavish painting of the Madonna and Child adorned the ceiling of the auditorium. Attached to the walls of the balcony was a series of decorative pillars which supported statues of girls wearing short dresses. These figures held bugles which would sound when they were announcing the coming attractions, but they didn't last long as one of the company's directors objected to their presence and ordered their removal. However, the pillars still remain in Screen 1 of the Cineplex today.

Eddie McGrath, a gentleman from Clonmel, was appointed the first manager of the Capitol. He grew up with cinemas in his blood as he had worked in his father's film business since he was a boy. The chief operator, Jack Finn, had been transferred from the

Capitol Theatre in Dublin to supervise the new staff. His assistants were Paddy Garrett, Ambrose Kelly, Henry Regan and Michael Creedon. The team of ushers was lead by Bartholomew Connery, along with Jack Davis and Cornelius Callaghan. Among the other staff who worked there in the early days were Betty Mangan whose brother John was a projectionist in the Lee, Bobby Byrne who went on to become an operator at the Coliseum,

Mr. Eddie McGrath

and Renee Dinan who over the years rose through the ranks to become the cinema's assistant manager.

THE FILMS ON DISPLAY at the Capitol merited the very finest in presentation, and their operating system was one of the best in the country. With the contract to show films from the studios of 20th Century Fox, Paramount and later Warner Brothers, they had the rights to such classics as the Alan Ladd western *Shane,* the POW comedy-drama *Stalag 17,* and their first CinemaScope picture *The King of the Khyber Rifles* which was shown in 1954. 20th Century Fox pioneered a new magnetic sound system to accompany CinemaScope, and the Capitol had the only one of its kind in Munster. The speakers, which were positioned on both sides of the screen and distributed around the house, produced amazing effects. For the first show a select audience of the staffs' friends and family were invited. Because the sound was so realistic, several children ran out crying when thunder broke out in the film.

Religious pictures were always very popular with the public, and none proved more appealing than Cecil B DeMille's 1956 version of *The Ten Commandments.* This was one of the most extravagant Hollywood productions of the day, and featured a huge cast led by Charlton Heston as Moses. No expense was spared with the sets or the costumes, and the special effects that were used for the parting of the Red Sea and the writing of the tablets were the most spectacular yet seen on film. However, one of its most unique and daring features was the personal appearance that Cecil B. DeMille made at the start of the picture. He emerged from behind a curtain and spoke directly to the audience, telling them where and how the film was made, and how they researched the script. This was a very radical move for a director, and Mr. DeMille's actions caused one of the Capitol's lady customers quite a bit of confusion. After the show one evening, one of the operators went down to the foyer where he was approached by a patron. 'Excuse me,' she said, 'where can I meet Cecil B. DeMille?' He replied 'Oh ma'am, I presume if you write care of Paramount Studios, Hollywood, USA.' 'Oh, no, no, no, no,' she said, 'where can I meet him personally?' The operator looked at her bewildered. 'I don't know,' he said, 'I don't know where he is.' She asked 'Where is he staying in Cork?' and he replied 'He's not in Cork ma'am?' Then she responded 'But he came out and spoke before the show started!'

IN THE SUMMER OF 1956 a polio epidemic swept through Cork city. To prevent the disease from spreading, all young people were banned from going to the cinemas. Because of this, a young man called John O'Leary from Douglas was refused entry to the Capitol one Friday as a customer, yet he was admitted the following Monday when he turned up for his first day of work as an apprentice operator. John was a big fan of live theatre and had found an ideal job as a programme seller in the Opera House. However, he lost his lovely job when that building burned down in December 1955. When he went to work in the Capitol some months later, it was one of a number of venues in Cork that was capable of holding live performances. The cinema contained a very big stage that was hidden from public view behind the screen, and there was a fly gallery above with a scenery door at the rear. The Cork Symphony Orchestra and the Cork Ballet Company both performed there, and it was used as a venue for the annual Pioneer School's concerts. Jimmy O'Dea once did a show there as well. However, after the widescreen was erected for CinemaScope, it was no longer possible to use the stage.

The Road Show Presentations were the cinema's biggest attraction during John's time working in the Capitol. These were the most lavish pictures of their day, made to impress audiences who were increasingly abandoning the big screen in favour of the small. The film company would take over the cinema for the duration of the movie's run, and would conduct extravagant promotional campaigns to capture the attention of the public. When the studios were running the show, normal in-house procedures were suspended. Alfred Hitckcock's *Psycho* was shown at the Capitol in the early 1960s, and it came with the instruction that nobody was to be admitted to the auditorium after the film had started. Tickets for the great epics like *The Longest Day, My Fair Lady, South Pacific,* and *Oliver!* were in huge demand, but the downside of these presentations was that the admission prices went up too. However, the biggest film ever shown at the Capitol was *The Sound of Music,* the romantic musical based on the real life story of the Von Trapp family, which starred Julie Andrews and Christopher Plummer. It ran for three months in 1967 and was the most successful film ever to play in a Cork cinema.

As an apprentice operator John learned all the tricks of the trade, and as employee of the Capitol from the 1950s to the 1970s, he witnessed all the main events in its history. One notable incident was a night in 1962 when there were major floods in Cork. The waters came right up the Grand Parade and reached the steps of the cinema. Some of the patrons had to be rescued by lorry that evening. Even after the floods had subsided, it still took weeks for the auditorium to be dried out. However, no date in that period stuck in his mind more than the night of November 22nd 1963. "You can always remember where you were when Kennedy died, because it was one of these events in history. Myself and another projectionist were up in the operating box when the door was swung open and Billy Joyce, the first usher, shouted in 'Here, Kennedy's been shot!' and we said 'What?' and he said 'Kennedy's been shot' and he ran out again." Because Billy Joyce was a bit of a prankster they didn't take any notice initially, but when they phoned the ticket desk, the cashier Betty Mangan confirmed that Kennedy had indeed been shot.

To alert the attention of the crowd when a big event like that had happened, the operators would write out a message on a glass slide and impose it over the main picture. As a film could not be interrupted, this method was often used to locate a member of the audience in an emergency, or to pass on the result of a big sporting event. That night they projected the message 'PRESIDENT KENNEDY SHOT IN DALLAS'. The whole of Cork went into mourning for the late President who had been in the city just three months earlier as part of his state visit to Ireland. As a mark of respect, the cinema closed its doors the following day.

LONG BEFORE IT WAS converted into a multiplex, the Capitol had operated two screens under the one roof. When it was first built in 1947, it came equipped with a restaurant which - in spite of its great location - never took off and was closed in the early 1950s. That space was subsequently used as an office and as the Press Club for the Film Festival, but it was transformed into a 105 seater screen called the Mini Capitol in December 1974. This provided a new attraction for the cinema, and in the first week large numbers turned up to see the George Lucas film *American Graffiti.* Big films whose business was starting to decline, and small films that didn't have the commercial appeal to fill the large house wound up at the Mini. However, it was viewed with disdain by some because it didn't have the size or the glamour of the other cinemas. 2 FM DJ Michael Cahill grew up in Cork, and for his birthday each year he would bring a group of friends to the cinema. One year he was all set to take them to a western called *Silverado,* but when he found out it was showing in the Mini he was so disgusted he brought them to something else instead. Despite the public's disregard for the Mini, it still survives virtually unchanged as Screen 6 of the Cineplex.

The 1970s were a revolutionary time in Hollywood. Following the collapse of the studio system, a new generation of directors emerged making modern and exciting films that drew massive audiences all around the world. Among these were *The Godfather* parts I and II, *Jaws, One Flew Over the Cuckoo's Nest, The Exorcist* and *Close Encounters of the Third Kind,* which enjoyed extended runs in the Capitol during that decade. Because these films were bold and daring, many of them contained controversial material that the censor saw fit to remove. Pat Mulcahy remembers going to see the Warren Beatty film *Shampoo* in the Capitol in the 1970s. The film arrived in Dublin and opened on a Friday, and due to the anticipated popularity, a second copy was ordered for Cork. The additional print, which came directly from Columbia Studios in Hollywood, was uncensored when it was screened in the Capitol for the first time the following Sunday. Pat went along a few days later, only to be told by one of the staff that he was a day late. They showed the full unedited version on the first night, but when some crank went to see it on the Monday, he complained about the content to the censor, Dermot Breen, who was living on the Model Farm Road at the time. Mr. Breen came into the Capitol the following day and made recommendations to remove certain sections.

TV personality Simon Williams in the company of Capitol employee Mrs. Barbara Cremin at the 1976 Film Festival. Mrs. Cremin's daughter, Barbara Dunne, still works in the Capitol Cineplex. Courtesy of Irish Examiner

FOLLOWING THE RETIREMENT of the long standing manager Eddie McGrath in 1981, Fred Hill came to the Capitol to take over

Mr. Fred Hill

the top job. Mr. McGrath had overseen the running of the cinema since it opened in 1947, so Fred had large shoes to fill. A former teacher and a keen photographer, Fred was in his own words a "complete blow-in to the cinema business". His first day on the new job was especially daunting. "It was like a scene from *Rebecca* where all the staff were lined up to meet the newcomer. It was a harrowing experience, everybody knowing more about the cinema business than I did. Oh it was very intimidating." It took him just a short time to adjust to his new surroundings, and when he did he took to it like a duck to water. "Everyday was a new day, and everyday you met new people and you had new experiences."

The business went through a very rough series of peaks and valleys during Fred's first few years, and the number of people who went to the Capitol depended entirely on the film that was being shown. The big hits in the 1980s included the epic Indiana Jones adventures *Raiders of the Lost Ark* and *The Temple of doom, Ghostbusters, Beverly Hills Cops, Top Gun* and the *Star Wars* movies. However the film that caused the greatest amount of pandemonium for the staff was *Santa Claus: The Movie* at Christmas in 1985. Fred frequently had to deal with unruly behaviour amongst people in the queues, but this film provoked an incident without precedent. At the time there were a lot of teachers strikes, and on one Wednesday afternoon all the children in Cork got an unexpected half day. When the staff arrived in for the matinee show they were confronted with a large angry mob of impatient school children desperate to get inside. "It was the case that on that particular afternoon every kid in Cork wanted to see the film and they all converged on the Capitol. We didn't even know there was going to be a strike. It was unexpected and we were caught totally unaware. At the start we had to form a human barricade in order to get in. We had to join hands and pull ourselves along. Then we made an announcement that there would be no show that afternoon, at which stage most of the people went away and we had a show for those who stayed."

The Capitol and the Mini continued to function as one of the main cinemas in Cork until 1989, when the plans for its conversion into the city's first multiplex were finally put into effect. Although such a scheme had been in the pipeline for years, it materialised in January of 1989 when the cinema closed for a lengthy period of reconstruction and renovation. The following August the new six screen cinema opened for business. Fred Hill and Donal Kelly were appointed managers of the new complex, and many of the staff members from the old cinemas joined the ranks as well. The new Cineplex proved to be as popular with the people of Cork in 1989 as the original one had been in 1947. Fred recalls that "people were dying to get in, and we saw things we had never seen before like queues in the afternoon...Not only had we two films running there, but we now had six. So there would always be something of interest." Donal stayed there until 1995 when he retired after forty eight years employment in Cork cinemas, but sadly Fred's career was cut short in 1992 due to illness. He enjoyed the eleven years he worked in the Capitol, and his only regret was "that it was so short."

3. HOUSES OF RESURRECTION

NOT EVERYONE COULD afford the price of a ticket to the Savoy's Grand Circle, and furthermore, not everyone was sufficiently well connected to get tickets for the prime first run features on Sunday nights in any of the main cinemas. However, back in those days, people got a second chance to see films if they missed them first time around. Today, films are distributed to cinemas for a short intensive period and make the transition to video six months later. This was not the case in the past when there were a series of 'second-run' picture houses showing Hollywood entertainment several months after their outing at the larger cinemas. Cork had three venues where patrons could enjoy films a second time round for cheaper prices. They were the Coliseum on MacCurtain Street, the Lee on Winthrop Street, and the Ritz on Washington Street.

THE COLISEUM
Cork's First Cinema

THE COLISEUM CINEMA, which occupied the corner of MacCurtain Street and Brian Boru Street, holds the unique privilege of being the first to be custom built in Cork for the purpose of showing pictures. The premises which were entirely funded with Irish money and constructed by local firms, opened to a rapturous reception on Tuesday the 9th of September 1913. Owned by Southern Coliseums Ltd, it showed the most elaborate and up to date pictures in the city. The cinema also had the most modern projection equipment. This guaranteed that films could be watched in all their glory without any of the unsteadiness that was quite common in other picture houses. On the first night the chairman of Southern Coliseums, Mr. David Frame, took to the stage and assured the large audience of local dignitaries and influential people that the management of the new cinema would do all in their power to show the best and brightest films that were available. The first manager was Mr. M. J. Tighe, who had previous experience in the business having been in charge of the Imperial Cinema in Cobh for a short period.

The Coliseum. Courtesy of Irish Examiner

Throughout its early years the Coliseum drew an audience of discriminating moviegoers, and it was always considered to be a high class auditorium where the crowd never caused any trouble. However, the forces of history conspired against the Col and brought it into the firing line during one of the bleakest periods in Irish history. On the evening of December 11th 1920, several shots were fired between the British armed forces and Irish rebels outside the cinema on the corner of MacCurtain Street, however there were no casualties. Later that night, vast portions of the city centre were burned to the ground by the Black and Tans. According to the late

Stanley Cant who was the manager of the Col between 1947 and 1964, during the War of Independence the IRA allegedly took over the building and operated it for their own purposes. It was understood that they took ultimate control of the finances and kept the door receipts to fund their military campaign.

Business returned to normal after the troubles ended, and in 1925, Mr. Tighe's eventful time as manager came to an end. He was replaced by Mr. Brett who, in turn, was succeeded by Mr. Norwood two years later. The Coliseum continued to be one of the most prominent picture houses in the city during the 1920s, and it gained this reputation because of the top notch films on offer. These included Cecil B. DeMille's original version of *The Ten Commandments* which was made in 1923, the spectacular 1926 film of *Ben Hur,* and another DeMille religious epic entitled *King of Kings* which ran for several weeks in 1929.

Paddy Buckley worked in the Coliseum as an usher in the 1930s and 1940s, and he remembers the unique experience of visiting that cinema during the silent days. Before the films started to talk, the theatres had to improvise for sound and the Col came equipped with its own team of sound effects experts. They would stand at the side of the screen and pop papers bags, rattle tin cans, chains, and other artefacts at appropriate parts of the film. Music was also one of the prime attractions. As well as having a small live orchestra who provided the musical accompaniment to go with the picture, on Sunday nights a man from Piggot's Record Shop on Patrick Street would take centre stage thirty minutes before the start of the film and play gramophone records to entertain the audience.

Opera seasons were also a regular speciality of the Coliseum's programme in the 1920s. Two of the finest productions of the time were 'Lily of Killarney' and 'Carmen', which were staged by the Bowyer Westwood Company. Albert Bowyer and Olive Westwood, the company's directors and principal players, were also the grandparents of the popular singer and Royal Showband member Brendan Bowyer. Olive Westwood had an impressive mezzo soprano voice and was regarded as one of the best incarnations of Carmen in her day. Over the next thirty years the Coliseum was occasionally used as a venue for live recitals and concerts. Their greatest show was held in the summer of 1953 when the Cork Grand Opera Group staged their spectacular production of Vincent Wallace's 'Maritana'. The famous English tenor Heddle Nash played the lead role, with the soprano Eugenie Castle in support. The show featured a sixty person chorus and an

Programme for the 1953 production of 'Maritana'

orchestra of twenty under the leadership of W.E. Brady, and for this epic performance, a special stage and lighting system was constructed. It was a production of the highest quality and received wide praise from both the public and critics alike.

THE STYLE AND decorations of the Coliseum's interior were based on the tomb of the Egyptian King Tutankhamon, and it had very good acoustics because most of the auditorium was covered in wooden panels. Seating 700 people, the Col was designed as a stadium cinema which meant everyone was guaranteed a good view of the screen. It was divided into three sections, the cheapest of which was the 4d hop by the front. This was a popular haunt for children and the unwaged. The second section was slightly more tapered and more expensive than the one before, while the dearest seats were at the rear of the house. In the evening this part was well frequented by couples, both young and old alike. Young lovers were especially attracted to the charms of the Col as it was a nice clean, comfortable cinema which was blissfully free of fleas. In addition, for most fellows taking their girlfriends out on a date it was more affordable than the Savoy or the Pavilion. Although the courting couples craved the privacy of the Col's most exclusive section, their romantic clinches were often disturbed by the ushers flashing their torches at anyone who was 'misbehaving'.

For much of its life the Coliseum specialised in second run features, or as they were known in Cork, 'resurrections'. The management would check the receipts from the first run cinemas to see which pictures did the most business, and they would book the best films some time after their initial release. Reissued musicals and westerns were always a winner, as were the comedies of Laurel and Hardy, Abbot and Costello, Bing Crosby and Bob Hope, and the Marx Brothers. The cinema had three showings a day, and the programme changed three times a week on Mondays, Thursdays and Sundays. If a second run film was popular, a lot of its fans would go back again to have another look, but there were many distractions to deal with when someone went to see a reissued film for the first time. Donal Kelly from the Pavilion went to see Christopher Lee's *Dracula* on its return visit to Cork as he had missed it first time around. Unfortunately for him, many of the others in the cinema were experiencing the terror for the second time. "There were two girls behind me who had seen it before and they were giving a commentary on it." There was always some person who would shout out 'he's going to kill her now' at the appropriate moment and spoil the suspense for the first timers. "I turned around and said 'Would you ever shut up. I'm only seeing this picture for the first time.'"

The queues for the Coliseum were so long they regularly reached all the way down Brian Boru Street to the quay, and it often got rough as people tried to push their way in. When the house was full the ushers would try to close the doors, but there was always some jostling from members of the crowd frantic to get one of the last seats. Fergal Crowley, who spent half of his working life in The Munster Arcade, preferred the Col to any of the other cinemas and was a frequent visitor from the 1940s to the 1960s. "There were fierce queues that time. I remember we'd go to the matinee, and if you were unlucky enough to be in the front row it would be difficult to see the film because the screens were smaller and all the figures appeared oblong and egg shaped. This was before CinemaScope came in." Incidentally, the Munster Arcade made the staff uniforms for the Col, the Pavilion and the Palace.

Children represented a huge portion of the Coliseum's customers, and Saturday afternoon was their special day. Fire regulations were rarely observed as the kids were packed in three or four to a seat, sat on the steps, or stood in any patch of available space. Marie Nash who worked there as an usherette in the 1950s and 1960s has fond memories of the great atmosphere at the Saturday matinees. "There was an awful lot of poverty among the children, but in the cinema they were so happy. Pictures were great for the children because they forget all their problems." It took them to a different world. When the film came on the kids appeared entranced by what was happening on the screen, and they never took any notice of the ushers walking around them. The most memorable picture for Marie was the western *Davy Crockett,* which featured a famous song that was doing the rounds at the time. When it came on in the course of the film, all the children started singing it at the tops of their voices. The noise they made was so intense that when she went on her break, she could still hear them singing from up the street. "I thought they'd lift the roof."

One of the principal reasons the Col was such a popular venue with young people, and is still so fondly remembered today, was because of their annual children's matinee at noon on St. Stephen's Day. On the day after Christmas each year, children from all over the city would head for the Col flush with money from 'doing the wran' earlier in the morning. The management always presented a good programme which featured the likes of Mickey Mouse cartoons, Three Stooges shorts, and a cowboy film like Hopalong Cassidy or Roy Rogers. However the greatest attraction of this show was that every child got a free bag of sweets courtesy of the cinema. The staff were similarly rewarded at Christmas time when Hadji Bey, the owner of the famous sweet shop on MacCurtain Street, supplied each of them with a box of Turkish Delights. Mr. Bey was a regular visitor to the Col as he rented space under the stage where he stored some of his merchandise. He frequently called in to chat to the workers and might watch half an hour of the film in the process.

IN 1955 FRANK NASH joined the staff of the Col as a fourteen year old apprentice operator. He quickly found himself becoming a part of the family of people who worked there and who shared in its triumphs and tragedies. Stanley Cant was the manager when

Frank joined and had been in the job since 1947. Mr. Cant, whose family were shareholders in Southern Coliseums Ltd, grew up in the business and had a great knowledge and fondness for cinemas. Mr. Newman, who hailed from Magazine Road, was the chief projectionist. Before moving into the cinema business, Mr. Newman owned an

Mr. Stanley Cant electrical shop and had also been a keen ham radio enthusiast. He was strongly opposed to all forms of censorship, and the Coliseum never showed the censor's certificate when he was in charge. As his apprentice, it was Frank's responsibility to remove the censor's stamp from the start of each show.

Frank quickly learned his trade as an operator, but like everyone in that profession he had to endure his share of breakdowns. "It happened to me on many occasions as it happened to all projectionists." When the breakdowns occurred there would be roaring and bawling and stamping and shouting from the crowds, and the phones would start ringing in the box as the ushers urged the operators to get the show back on the road. Often the reason why the picture broke down was because the joints holding the film together had snapped. One of the duties of the projectionists was to make sure all the joints were secure, so they had to run the film between their thumb and forefinger to feel if it was well assembled. Consequently, for years afterwards Frank had no fingerprints.

Many of the Col's staff had been there since the silent days, so when Frank arrived he went to work alongside some people who had been in the business long before he was born. Kay Kiely was the cinema's principal cashier, and she was one of their longest serving employees. In the 1950s she introduced a very unique feature to the Col. The cinema had a number of dressing rooms that dated back to the days when they held live shows, but by the 1950s they were no longer in use. Miss Kiely who was a very religious person, received permission from Mr. Cant the manager to turn one of them into a chapel. An altar was installed and the rosary was said there every day at 2pm just before the start of the first show. All staff were expected to attend, and Miss Kiely would give out to anyone who wasn't present. Once a year a priest came over from St. Patrick's Church across the road and said mass for the staff.

The time spent in the Coliseum was productive and rewarding for Frank, and it set him in good standing for the rest of his life. His boss, Mr. Newman, was a very learned man who introduced Frank to a world of books, and encouraged him to return to his education. He also became involved with the cinema's trade union, and was at one time the youngest shop steward in the city. This was the beginning of his long life in local politics. He later went on to join the Labour Party, was elected to the Cork Corporation, and served a term as Lord Mayor. Like all people working in the cinema business he developed a good knowledge of films, but in his time at the Col he rarely got to see one from

Marie and Frank Nash

beginning to end. Each operator had their own 20 minute reel to show, and when it was finished they could sit down and read or have a cup of tea. Today when he watches an old movie, Frank sees pieces he never saw before as it wasn't part of his 20 minutes. However, the most important life changing experience for him was meeting a young lady called Marie who started work in the Col in 1958 as an usherette. They started courting shortly afterwards and got married several years later. They remain happily together to this day.

A BUS STOP CONVENIENTLY located outside the cinema brought business in from lots of people living on the Lower Road, Mayfield, Dillon's Cross and other parts of the North East of the city. Many of them were tempted to go into the Col when they got off the bus saw the posters for the films. However when CIE moved the stop further back on MacCurtain Street to the Metropole in the early 1960s, much of the Col's business went with it. Mr. Cant contacted CIE and pleaded with them to bring the stop back to its original spot but to no avail. Then television arrived and the crowds started to decline drastically. The old picture house tried to weather the storm, but by the end of March 1964 its fate could no longer be avoided. After a meeting of the company's directors in Dublin, it was decided to call it a day. With a screening of *The Man in the Iron Mask,* the cinema closed unceremoniously on the night of April 4th, 1964.

THE LEE
"You Can Rely on the Lee"

AS FAR AS cinemas in Cork go, the Lee was always something of an anomaly. If picture houses had been entered into a race, the Lee would have been an also ran. It rarely showed the biggest films on their initial releases, it didn't boast the luxury or splendour of the majestic Savoy across the road, nor does it strike up passionate memories for its former patrons as do places like the Palace, the Pavilion or even the Imperial. However, each cinema had a

The Lee Cinema

character all of its own and the Lee on Winthrop Street was no different from the others in that respect. It opened quietly on Monday, November 1st 1920, at a time when the city was entrenched in the violence from the War of Independence. The Lord Mayor Terrence MacSwiney had died on hunger strike the week before, so patronising a new picture house was hardly at the top of most people's agendas.

However, less than six weeks later, the fledgling cinema was caught up in one of Cork's greatest tragedies. Following an ambush at Dillon's Cross, K Company of the Black and Tans ran riot through the centre of the city setting fire to many of the major businesses and stores. Most of the eastern side of Patrick Street was burned to the ground, with landmarks like Roches Stores and the Muster Arcade being completely destroyed. The fire in Cashes, the building adjoining the Lee, swept into the cinema gutting its interiors entirely, although its facade was left miraculously intact. It was the only building to stay standing amidst the charred relics of the rest of Patrick Street. After considerable refurbishment, it reopened nine months later on Thursday, September 22nd, 1921. Its first picture was called *Slaves of Pride,* a silent film starring Alice Joyce and Percy Marmint, and the Bradys, a prominent Cork musical family, provided live orchestral accompaniment.

Seating just four hundred and fifty people, the Lee was one of the smallest and cosiest cinemas in the city centre, and it had an Old World charm that it retained for most of its long life. It is famously remembered by many for being one of the easiest cinemas to duck into without paying. Because it was renowned for being dark and dingy, it was also an especially popular hideout for people who were on the lang from school. It had a cash desk out front facing the street, with a winding staircase on the right which led up to the balcony. In addition, there were two old fashioned doors at either side of the ticket box going into the stalls. As there was usually only one person in the box and one usher guarding the doors, it was sometimes possible for a daring youngster to sneak in through the other entrance unnoticed by staff. Sometimes they were lucky and got in for free, but if they picked the wrong door they was a chance they might run up against an usher called Luke Collins who was waiting inside to catch those who didn't have tickets.

Miss Madge O'Regan and Mrs. Julia Scraggs were the owners of the Lee. Both were prominent business women in the city, and Mrs. Scraggs in particular had many property interests around Cork. Together they ran a successful and popular little cinema which was advertised with the slogan 'You Can Rely On The Lee'. In December 1929, it became only the third picture house in the city to convert to sound, and its first talkie was the colour Warner Brothers musical *On with the Show*. It was also one of the first picture houses to install air conditioning.

In August of 1931, the Lee was the first cinema in Cork to screen the classic horror film *Dracula* which became one of their biggest hits. Hundreds of people were turned away on the opening night alone. Those that were admitted were shocked and terrified by the spooky figure of Count Dracula as he emerged from the fog in the dead of night to suck the blood of young maidens. Bela Lugosi played the role of the infamous vampire and his appearance on screen sent people in the audience into shrieks of terror. In order to prove how brave they were, many young boys would go to a horror film alone and then pretend they weren't disturbed when they came out later. As often as not they were lying, as they had spent much of the film with their hands over their eyes or hiding under the seat. In contrast to the horror of *Dracula*, the charming, innocent pictures of child star Shirley Temple were another top attraction at the Lee during the 1930s.

ONE OF THE MOST famous and popular managers of the Lee was Sidney Crewe from Turner's Cross, and he cycled to work everyday wearing a navy blue suit and a bowler hat. The office in which he worked was little bigger than a phone booth, yet that never dampened his spirits. He was a thorough gentleman who was very well liked by his staff, and he had a welcoming smile for all the customers. In Mr. Crewe's early years at the Lee, electricity was

rationed because of the Second World War. Consequently most cinemas were restricted to showing just one film a day. However, the Lee was able to survive because they had their own DC generator. Everyday the meter reader from the ESB would arrive to check that the cinema wasn't using more than its allotted units, so the chief operator would turn the generator down to the very lowest point where it could still supply enough juice to power the carbon arc lamps in the projectors. By doing this he managed to keep within the allowed units, and so they could put on four screenings a day. However, all that appeared on the screen was a dirty brown blur.

Mr. Sidney Crewe

The cinema's operating box was nearly as small as Sidney Crewe's office. It jutted out past the façade of the building on Winthrop Street, and if it hadn't been for that extension the staff wouldn't have had any room at all. Mr. McGarry had been chief operator in the 1930s, and he was succeeded by Tim Murphy in the 1940s. Mr. Murphy and his wife were also the proprietors of a sweet shop on the Grand Parade. Willie Linnane from Douglas Street was second operator, and John O'Regan was third. Willie was one of three brothers who worked as operators in Cork cinemas, and their father had been the commisionaire in the Lee in the 1930s. In December 1942, a young man called Noel Ryan from St. Lukes joined the crew as the apprentice.

Because of the rationing of electricity during the war, the Lee had to forego some basic necessities such as lighting if they were to have enough energy to run the projectors. Four skylights were installed in the roof to allow natural light into the auditorium when it was being cleaned by day. These had to be closed prior to the beginning of the first show. As a junior operator it was Noel Ryan's job to go up on the roof, walk along the rafters and close the skylights by hand. One day at about five to three he was going up to do his duty, when he put his foot through the roof and sent a yard of plaster falling down into the 4d hops below. As these were the cheapest seats in the house they were normally the busiest, but as luck would have it they were quiet that day and nobody was hurt. Yet for Noel the situation was different. He remembers hanging down from the beams trying to hold on for dear life, as Sidney Crewe stared up at him with his mouth open in astonishment.

Many of the minor repairs had to be carried out by the apprentice as well, and an enormous amount of damage done to all the picture houses was caused by cigarette smoke. Before the introduction of the ban on smoking in cinemas, there were no restrictions where people could light up. The air would always be thick with cigarette and pipe smoke, and the sounds of coughing and spluttering were a regular feature of every show. The smoke turned the screens yellow and tarnished all the seats and the walls. The loudspeakers were positioned behind the screens which were perforated to let the sound flow through, but as the constant build up of smoke clogged up all the holes, the sound became very muffled. Screens were very costly to replace, so one day Noel and another projectionist got ladders, leaned them up against the screen and used

Noel Ryan

screwdrivers to unblock the perforations around the speakers. When they were finished and satisfied with their work, they walked back up the auditorium to look at the results. To their dismay what they saw was the same yellow screen – only this time it was full of holes too.

WHEN MRS. SCRAGGS and Miss O'Regan decided to sell their interests in the Lee in the 1950s, they gave the first offer to Abbey

71

Films, the company owned by Leo Ward and Kevin Anderson. Abbey Films had supplied many pictures to cinemas around the country during that decade, and the Lee was one of their primary clients in Cork. Among the films that sold many tickets in that period were the comic antics of Dean Martin and Jerry Lewis, Norman Wisdom, and Abbott and Costello, although it was the arrival of Rock and Roll that proved to be the biggest sensation of the time. The Bill Haley film *Rock Around the Clock* first played in Cork in the Pavilion in July 1956, and it returned to the Lee just three months later. This had been a very controversial film on its initial release, and many theatre owners were slow to book it as they were worried it might provoke trouble as it had in England. No such scenes occurred in Cork on its first run, but when the picture was shown in the Lee second time around, the enthusiastic crowd started jiving in the aisles of the cinema as the hip rhythms of the new groovy music were played in the film. Another rock movie *Shake, Rattle and Roll* played there in February 1957 with similar results.

Not long after taking over, Ward and Anderson employed the services of a man named Michael John O'Sullivan, whose face is familiar to anyone who went to the cinema in Cork in the latter half of the 20th Century. He is the longest surviving member of the business, and he started his career as a twelve year old pageboy in the Pavilion back in 1947. He responded to an ad which specified a boy that was 'small, smart and smiling', and during the interview his fingernails and posture were examined by the manager Kevin O'Donovan. After seeing off much competition, he got the job starting at five shillings a week. His special uniform consisted of a pillbox hat, a short jacket with plastic buttons and short trousers, and he was put in charge of the cloakroom where he received very good tips from the customers. His mother Mary O'Sullivan was the carver in the Pav's restaurant for forty years, but he got the job there unbeknownst to her. It was only after she met him in uniform that she found out he was working there too. He stayed on at the Pav after he left school and was promoted to the job of usher. Following a period of employment in other picture houses, he moved to the Savoy around the time of the first Film Festival. There he remained until he was offered the job in the Lee across the road.

Michael John started his work in the Lee as the commisionaire. In his early days, there were iron gates at the exterior of the cinema which offered the staff little protection from the weather. He said "You'd be blown out of the Lee standing at the front of the house when you'd be checking tickets." Later doors were installed and he was able to work inside away from the eye of the storm. Sidney Crewe was still in charge during Michael John's first few years, and when he retired in June of 1964 after more than two decades of distinguished service, the staff and management of all the other cinemas paid tribute to the professional and courteous manner with which he conducted himself in the job. He was replaced by Stanley Cant who had previously been manager of the Coliseum, and who was employed by Abbey Films after it closed in 1964. Mr. Cant also had troubleshooting responsibilities in the Palace and the Pavilion, but his main duties resided in the Lee. From the beginning, he and Michael John forged a strong working relationship which lasted for more than twenty years.

IT WAS CLEAR THAT the cinema industry was entering very difficult times in the 1970s, and many houses around the country were hard hit for business. Lots of pubs and night clubs had opened and were drawing crowds away from the pictures, while the introduction of colour television gave people a further reason to stay at home. It appeared that smaller and more comfortable cinemas were best equipped to deal with the changing circumstances, so Abbey Films decided to downsize the Lee. The place closed on Saturday, April 8th 1972, and after seven months of changes and conversion, it was relaunched on Sunday, November 19th 1972, with a screening of the musical *Cabaret*. The building was divided in two and the new cinema was all contained on the upstairs floor. The ground section was turned into a shop. The walls of the auditorium and foyer were decorated with green curtains to give it a cosy feel, and luxurious single seats were installed, with jumbo armchairs in the tapered section at the back. In total the new cinema had a capacity for two hundred and fifty persons, but now that there was only one entrance, it was no longer possible for people to duck in for free.

For the remainder of its life, the Lee became the most important of all Cork's second run houses. They showed all the

bigger films after they had finished their run in the larger cinemas, and they sometimes revived popular older films as well. In the 1980s Michael John was promoted to the position of manager, and for the last few years of its life he ran the whole show in the Lee. His presence in that cinema was legendary and he enjoyed a great camaraderie with the customers. When the premises closed in August 1989 he moved to the new Capitol Cineplex where he was again employed as commisionaire, but the Lee would always be an important part of his life. Of his fifty year career he said "I enjoyed it, and I had many a

Michael John O'Sullivan

laugh and many a joke. The heartache and laughter goes with it. But it was worth it. If I had my life to start all over again I'd do the same...when you're happy in your job you can carry on regardless." He retired from the Capitol in 2001.

THE RITZ
Cork's Unluckiest Cinema

RUMOUR HAS IT that the portion of Washington Street on which the Ritz was located had at a time in the past been a fairy fort. Irish legend dictates that anything that is built on such sacred ground will bring bad luck to the owner. It seems as if the Ritz may have fallen foul of this misfortune. Masquerading under several different names, the Ritz as it was best known, was one of the mainstays of Cork's cinemas for over seventy years. Although it had to endure a fire, a rebuilding, and a few periods of closure, it survived until August of 1989 and was the last of all the old cinemas to close. Yet despite its longevity, it changed hands on four separate occasions and to each of the owners it brought a degree of bad luck.

In January of 1920, the Washington was the first cinema to open on that site. Although the street on which it stood was still formally known as Great George's Street, it was in the process of being changed to Washington Street and it was from this the cinema took its name. The Washington Cinema was small and squat, housing just over 300 people, yet uniquely it was heated by a coal fuel fire gate which was situated under the screen. It developed the reputation for being 'Cork's Cosiest Cinema' and made a point of advertising itself as such. However, like many picture houses of that era, it was frequented by as many fleas as paying customers. In the early 1930s, a young boy named Frankie Hayes from Albert Road sneaked into the Washington and sat down on one of long wooden benches that made up the cheaper downstairs section. Everyone knew when the film was about to start as a dot appeared on the screen, but before the beginning of the show an usher came into the auditorium with a can of Jeyes Fluid disinfectant to kill the fleas or the other germs that were floating about. "Your man came along with the disinfectant and poured it all along the floor and over everyone's shoes and anything else that might be there."

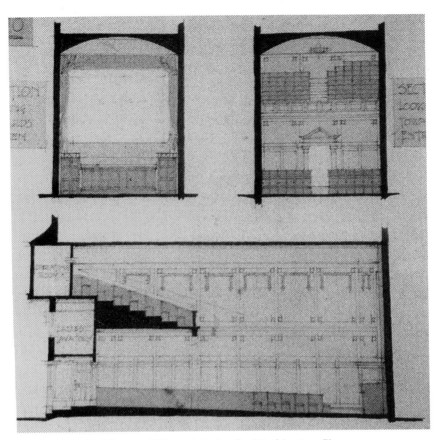

Architectural blueprints for the Washington Cinema.
Courtesy of the Cork Archives Institute Collection

Despite the smell of the Jeyes fluid and the presence of fleas, the Washington drew crowds from all over the city who were hungry for some big screen entertainment. They showed a lot of popular films of the day including those of cowboy heroes Tom Mix, Buck Jones and Ken Maynard, and comedy legend Charlie Chaplin. However, their biggest draw was Hollywood's greatest lover Rudolph Valentino. His films *The Four Horsemen of the Apocalypse, The Sheik* and *Blood and Sand* were always guaranteed to attract thousands of admiring females. Such was the appeal of his pictures that there was scarcely standing room available for many performances. In stark contrast to Valentino was Hollywood's scariest monster *King Kong*. Made in 1933, it was one of the most spectacular films ever produced. The great ape stunned and terrified the audiences of the Washington when he stormed in there on his first visit to Cork.

THE CURSE OF that cinema first hit early in the morning of Thursday, January 28th 1938, when the premises caught fire. The inferno, which started in the drapery shop of Messrs. O'Sullivan and Howard, spread rapidly into the cinema which was completely ablaze within an hour. A crowd of spectators gathered to watch the fire, but guards pushed them back for fear that the highly flammable films would cause an explosion. Robert McDonald, who worked for many years in the restaurant of the Savoy, watched the blaze from across the street in the arms of his mother when he was just a young boy. A courageous fireman charged into the burning building and rescued the films from the operators box which was located above the entrance hall. Superintendent Monaghan, the Chief of the Brigade, who was controlling operations on Tobin Street behind the cinema, just missed being hit by the rear wall and roof which collapsed in the blaze. Four families who were living in flats over the drapery shop escaped unharmed, and no one was injured by the fire which took over four hours to control. Nevertheless the cinema was completely destroyed, along with the shop and overlying flats, and the damage to the Washington was estimated at more than £4,000.

Stephen F. Whelan was the owner and managing director of the Washington cinema. He had been involved in cinemas in Cork since the early days, and in addition to owning the Washington, he was also the proprietor of the Imperial Cinema on Oliver Plunket Street and was at one time a director of the Lee. He was a qualified chemist by

Mr. Stephen Whelan

profession and was in partnership with the former Lord Mayor Sean French in the Whelan and French Pharmacy Shop on Patrick Street. After the fire in 1938, Mr. Whelan decided to build a different cinema on the same site, and formed a new company with the solicitor Thomas F. Meaghar. The adjoining premises that were destroyed in the blaze were purchased to facilitate the expansion of the new picture house, which opened on Sunday, August 13th, 1939. The first show was the heroic romance *Suez* which starred Tyrone Power. Tom Bryce, who was a former manager of the Coliseum, was put in charge of the new Ritz cinema.

The Ritz Cinema. Courtesy of Irish Examiner

With room for 590 persons, the Ritz was modestly sized but it was very awkwardly designed. The screen was very badly positioned because it was too high up for many of the people sitting downstairs, and it wasn't wide enough to provide a good view to the people sitting at the sides. Despite the fact that the balcony was sloped like the side of a mountain, the sight lines were much better for those sure footed persons who went up there. However these problems scarcely mattered as the Ritz had an exclusive contract to show all Warner Brothers films first run in Cork.

Warners were a company started by four brothers in 1923, and they turned out some of the most unforgettable films in Hollywood's history. During the Great Depression of the 1930s they were forced to cut back on budgets, and instead they turned out a string of inexpensive but extremely well made gangster films. These captured the public's imagination and brought forward a new generation of tough guy movie stars. *Little Caesar,* which starred Edward G. Robinson, and *Public Enemy* with the inimitable James Cagney, were the epitome of Warner Brothers low budget, high quality, hard boiled approach to film making. *Angels With Dirty Faces* produced the famous finale where Cagney cries for mercy as his character is about to be sent to the electric chair, while several years later he amazed audiences and critics with his performance as song and dance man George M. Cohan in *Yankee Doodle Dandy,* a film which won him an Oscar for Best Actor. The films of Errol Flynn, Bette Davis and Paul Muni similarly delighted the customers of the Ritz, but the most memorable star of all was a man who first came to people's attention as a contract player who was usually shot by Cagney in the final reel. His name was Humphrey Bogart.

During the 1940s, Bogie was the biggest attraction the Ritz had to offer. The queues for his films would frequently stretch as far as Singer's Corner on the Grand Parade. Bogart was as tough a tough guy as Cagney and Edward G. Robinson had been before him, but he was also a brave fighter against injustice and a charming ladies man. Of all the stars that endure from the golden age of movie making, perhaps none was greater than Bogart. He pottered around in films from the 1930s onwards, and by the end of that decade he had become well established in Warner Brothers films as a villainous character player. Yet it wasn't until 1941 that he got his breakthrough as a leading man in *High Sierra.* Later that year he moved a little closer to immortality when he played private eye Sam Spade in the classic detective film *The Maltese Falcon.* These two pictures established Bogart as a big star, and it was his standing with the public that led to him being cast in his most famous role of all – Rick Blaine in *Casablanca.* The next few years saw Bogart feature in many other time honoured films like *The Treasure of the Sierra Madre, To Have and Have Not* – the first film he made with his future wife Lauren Bacall – and *The African Queen,* for which he won an Oscar.

The Ritz had two stars of their own in the shape of the chief ushers Marky Holland and Paddy Ring. They ruled the roost with an iron fist and tolerated no nonsense from anyone. The pair became known throughout the city as Mutt and Jeff. Marky Holland in particular had a serious problem with the courting couples, and because the Ritz provided double seating which young lovers found especially appealing, he was kept busy trying to preserve moral decency in his establishment. Pat Mulcahy who regularly visited all the picture houses in Cork remembers seeing Marky in action one evening. "All the courting couples used to go to the Ritz and sit downstairs. Marky would walk up around the front by the screen, down one aisle and then back up again. Then he stood around for a bit and waited, and the next thing he put the lights on in the cinema and went and stood at the top by the screen. He looked down – and of course we all looked around – and there was a few courting couples in the back row. He went up to them and threw them out the door – but he'd really show them up before he'd throw them out." Other times he might not be as severe. He'd merely separate the lovers and seat one of them at the front of the house where he could keep an eye on them.

Marky was truly the enemy of young love, yet he was a man who could be beaten if you played your cards properly. John O'Shea from Fair Hill was one person who managed to get the better of that terrifying usher. "One Saturday night my two friends and I went to confession. After confession we decided to walk down town. We walked up Washington Street and stopped outside the Ritz. First we were looking at pictures on the display case as the usher was standing inside the door." They carefully bided their time, and when Marky left his post, the three of them ducked into the back row to watch Errol Flynn in *The Charge of the Light Brigade*. "The next morning we were nervous about going to communion after our 'crime' the night before."

THE CURSE HIT again in the 1950s when the Ritz lost the Warner Brothers contract to the Capitol. However, they managed to avoid financial disaster by switching to continental films in December of 1956. At that time the government had introduced a new tax on pictures, but foreign films were exempt because they were deemed to be educational. Many of the new pictures on show were of the highest artistic standards, including those of Italian film maker Frederico Fellini and Swedish director Ingmar Bergman. *Sissi,* a series of films about Princess Elizabeth of Bavaria, ran for many weeks at a time in the 1950s, while *The Trapp Family,* the original German film that would later be the subject for *The Sound of Music,* was one of their biggest hits under this new policy. These accomplished pictures drew large crowds of serious filmgoers, but many others they showed were a bit raunchy for the time and proved to be very popular with adolescent males and the 'raincoat' brigade. The films of French sex symbol Brigitte Bardot and others like her generated queues like Bogart's films had done in the 1940s, but because the censor's knife was so sharp in those days, it was rare for something remotely offensive or racy to make it to the screen.

Sadly the source of these films dried up in the early 1960s, forcing the cinema to show outdated material that didn't manage to attract many customers. Stephen Whelan, the Ritz's long standing managing director and principal shareholder, died in February of 1963, leaving the cinema without its spiritual leader. Following his death, the cinema met with many troublesome times and it was finally sold to the Dublin based Amalgamated Cinemas (Ireland) Ltd. in August of 1966. The directors of this company were the Elliman family, who owned theatres throughout the country, and several members of the family served on the board of directors for the J. Arthur Rank Cinemas, who controlled the Savoy cinemas in Cork and Dublin. They invested heavily in the modernisation of the Ritz, but during their period in charge they faced many of the same problems as their predecessors. They had a big hit with the first run screening of *A Man for All Seasons* in 1968, and did good business with reissues of popular films like *The Sound of Music, Lawrence of Arabia* and the like. However television was quickly eating into the second run market, and in the long term the Ellimens couldn't make a success of the place. In February of 1974 they decided to close the Ritz. The curse once again had exacted revenge on any tenant who took up residency there.

WITHOUT SHOWING A FILM for nearly two years, the troubled premises enjoyed yet another lease of life when it was reopened by Seamus Quinn, who also owned and operated the Cameo on Military Road. Seamus had been in the business since 1948 when he started off as an apprentice operator in the Pavilion. In the 1950s, he worked in some of the main cinema chains in England, before returning to Ireland to set up his own business. He opened a picture house in Glanmire and also ran a travelling cinema which he brought to some of the main towns outside the city. In 1964 he converted the old Gaiety Ballroom on Military Road into the most technically modern cinema in the city. The prosperity of the Cameo in the decade that followed prompted him to expand his interests further. He acquired the Ritz from its previous owners and spent a considerable amount of money refurbishing and renovating the premises. It opened on Sunday the 28th of December 1975 under the new name, the Classic. Like its sister cinema the Cameo, it was an adult venue and no one under 21 was admitted.

Despite the huge time and resources he invested, Seamus was never able to generate the business he would have wished for. "I had terrible bad luck there and the people before me couldn't make a go of it either." In 1979, after just four years, he off-loaded the Classic to Abbey Films who kept it running throughout the 1980s. By the end of that decade it was one of just three of the old picture houses to remain in business, and for a few days in August of 1989 it was the only functioning cinema in Cork. When the evening screening of *Mississippi Burning* finished on August 10th, the cinema closed yet again. This time it would not reopen.

More than ten years later, long after the building had been demolished to make way for an apartment and office complex, Seamus Quinn was talking to a girl who had worked as a waitress in a restaurant on the site of the old cinema. Without knowing he was a former owner, she told him that she saw the transparent ghost of an old lady in the restaurant one evening. The ghost was sitting down and looking in the direction of where the screen used to be. As the supernatural elements continued to surface again, so too did the curse: the restaurant went out of business as well.

4. THE FLEAPITS

THE WORD FLEAPIT has little meaning anymore, but more than half a century ago 'fleapit' had a resounding significance for thousands of people. Basically translated as a small, dingy and often unhygienic cinema, the fleapits were the lowest of the low and then some, but what they lacked in comfort, they more than compensated with character. These were the haunts frequented by those who hadn't the money to sit in the luxurious surroundings of the Savoy or the Pavilion. There was no organ playing melodious tunes to a delighted audience. Forget any notions of a fancy restaurant where one could enjoy high tea before the film. In many cases, people were lucky if the projector didn't break down during the screening. And of course there were the fleas. They are an extinct breed now, but for scores of Cork people, the memory of sitting in the confined squalor of Miah's, or the ambient decadence of the Assems, are as pleasant and colourful as nights spent in the Grand Circle of the Savoy. One person aptly called them the 'speakeasies' of the cinema world. For many they were to be avoided like the plague. For others, they were the heart and soul of Cork.

THE ASSEMBLY ROOMS
"Georgie, remove the body!"

IT IS QUITE UNUSUAL for a cinema to have its origins in religious squabbles from the mid 19th century, yet that is exactly what happened in the case of the Assembly Rooms at No. 22 South Mall. Originally called the 'Protestant Hall and City And County of Cork Assembly Rooms', its beginnings came about when the Catholic powers in Cork denied permission to a renegade ex-priest named Fr. Gavazzi to deliver a lecture against Roman Catholicism in the Cork Athenaeum (the Opera House of the day). Many people in the city were greatly annoyed by this refusal, so a new hall was commissioned where the Catholic hierarchy would have no immediate influence. The Earl of Bandon laid the foundation stone of the new building on St. Patrick's Day in 1860, and he also performed the opening ceremony a year later on April 12th, 1861.

The Assems

Despite the somewhat sectarian beginnings of the Assembly Rooms, the premises opened in a spirit of toleration and continued to operate that way. The hall became one of the most fashionable venues in Cork during the latter half of the 19th century, playing host to boxing matches, speeches from the legendary Fenian

Jeremiah O'Donovan Rossa, temperance rallies from Father Matthew, and recitals from John McCormack. Composer Franz Listz visited the Assems while on an excursion to Cork, and many of the great opera companies of the day staged shows there. The premises were also the home of the Cork Literary and Scientific Society, and in 1910 their special guest was the son of Charles Dickens who gave a lecture on his father's works. Dickens himself had visited Cork in the 19th Century and had developed a great fondness for the city.

THE ASSEMBLY ROOMS had been in business for more than thirty five years before it started to engage in the activity for which it was best remembered. In April of 1896, moving pictures were shown there for the very first time as part of a fair in aid of the Munster Convalescent Home. In fact it was the first time pictures were shown in Cork. The premiere was a great success and 'Electric Living Pictures' became a regular feature of the Assembly Rooms' activities throughout the next decade. The technology that was first employed to show films was radically different from today, as the pictures were projected from behind the screen rather than from in front which would become the standard. Programmes of films were often shown at Christmas time, and the demand was so great that scores of people often failed to gain admission. Interestingly, in their programme for Christmas of 1908, some of the short films were able to talk and sing using a very crude form of sound recording and synchronisation.

During the next two decades silent films became the most popular form of entertainment around the world, and the Assems kept Cork crowds amused with all the latest films, cartoons, newsreels and sporting events. Although the movies may not have made any noise, that was where the silence ended. The pictures came with subtitled cards to explain to the audience what was going on, and slow readers would have to strain themselves to absorb all the information before it vanished from the screen. There was always a share of people who would read the titles out loud to assist the slow readers, but this infuriated the more serious film goers who wanted to see the picture in peace. The workings of the projector also contributed a great deal of clamour, but the clattering of the machinery was drowned out by the live accompanying piano music that was supplied by a lady called Cissie Kingsley. She played along in a manner which gave the silent films a voice. Underscoring every emotion and action with remarkable accuracy, she played lively, vibrant pieces when the action was taking place on the screen, yet reduced the tempo to a soothing melody when the picture turned its attention to romance.

The talkies came to the Assems in the early 1930s, and they were one of the last cinemas in Cork to get them. The installation of sound provided a new set of problems that was unique to the Assems, as the noise was so loud it could be heard in the adjoining Holy Trinity Church. Consequently the screen had to be moved to the other end of the hall closest to the South Mall. The madness and mayhem that had accompanied the silent pictures was a distraction when sound films arrived, and so a sign was posted over the entrance informing the customers that they now had to be quiet during the picture. Unsurprisingly no one ever took much notice, and the crowd continued to provide their own 'commentary' to go along with the films.

FOR THE YOUNG PEOPLE of the city, there was no greater place for excitement than the cinema they affectionately called the 'ass and belly Rooms'. On Saturday afternoons the half of Cork might turn up to get one of the 670 seats inside. This was the highlight of the week for many and they would scrimp, save and hustle to try and get enough money together to afford the price of a ticket. Crowds would gather in the street outside, and they'd push and shove and surge to try and get the best position when the doors opened. Inside was a hallway with a staircase in the middle, and people would queue up on the left of the stairs to go into the 4d hops. Positioned right up at the front by the screen, that was the cheapest section in the house and the seats comprised of long wooden benches. Eamonn McSweeney from Donnybrook started going to the pictures in the 1930s, and he remembers how there was often an almighty crush amongst the people who were jockeying for position when going into the 4d seats. "There were stairs on the side going into to the 4d place, and if there was a crush on and your arm got caught in the banisters, you'd nearly break it trying to get in."

The more expensive 9d and 1s 3d sections lay to the rear of the cinema, which was accessible via a very long corridor. That passageway was full of surprises, and customers making the treacherous odyssey to the dear seats had to pass old committee and games rooms that dated back to the Assems' early years, and the toilets which had a reputation for being amongst the smelliest in Cork. There was also a beautiful garden which belonged to the Capuchian Order next door, and all along the walls were photographs of old Hollywood stars. The corridor was so long that by the time you finally got to your seat, the picture was nearly over. The 9d division in the middle consisted of comfortable individual tip-up seats, while at the back of the house was the even more exclusive 1s 3d section. This was as luxurious and prestigious as the Assems got. It was slightly sloped to give everyone a good view, and it was a place only for those 'big shots' with money or with dates. Cork's 'rich and famous' hung out here, dressed to the nines in their navy blue overcoats and white scarves. People who were privileged enough to have the price for that part of the house would nearly expect the rest of the crowd to genuflect to them because of their importance.

The full programme at the Assems lasted for about two hours, and featured a trailer, ads, a few shorts and the main picture. Laurel and Hardy, the Three Stooges, Joe E. Brown and the Bowrey Boys were the great supporting attractions on the bill. There was a short interval before the main feature began, and in that time,

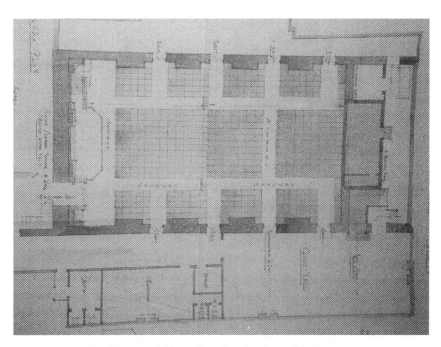

Architectural blueprints for the Assembly Rooms.
Courtesy of the Corᴸ Archives Institute Collection

Longitudinal Section

everyone rushed outside to the shop next door to buy the refreshments. These usually consisted of Scot's Clan, bulls eyes, aniseed balls and donkey's gudge. Those who could afford it brought in a few woodbines as well. The air of the Assems was so clouded with smoke that it was often difficult to see the screen, however cigarettes were very scarce and every last leaf of tobacco had to be cherished. One time a guy at the end of one row had a woodbine but no match, and so another fellow at the far end of the same row duly obliged him with a light. When the cigarette was lighting he passed it back, but as everyone in between had taken a drag, by the time it was returned to the first fellow it was nearly burned down to the butt. Startled by what occurred he roared 'What happened my cigarette?', and the response from all the others was 'We all just wanted to make sure it was lighting.'

B movies were the cinema's main attractions and nothing pleased their audience more than a good action picture. Swashbucklers like Errol Flynn and war heroes like Audie Murphy were always great favourites, but for excitement and adventure nothing beat the westerns. During the silent era westerns were the films that had the greatest appeal, but their popularity endured for many years after the advent of sound. The same story of good guys and bad guys could be moulded many times to make it new and fresh, and there was always plenty of chases and shoot outs to keep both young and old amused. Tom Mix, Buck Jones, Ken Maynard, Bob Steele and Tim McCoy were the big stars who rode tall in the saddle and defended the virtues of the old west from all the evil villains and intruders. When the lights went down at the start of the show there would be thunderous cheering, and the shouting and roaring from the audience never let up. The hero was always known as 'the boy', and deafening chants of 'come on the boy' would emerge from all corners of the house when he first rode across the screen. Right throughout the picture the crowd would scream out words of encouragement or warning to 'the boy' when the need arose.

Tom Mix was perhaps the biggest western star in the 1920s, and he was well acquainted with life in the old west having worked as a lumber jack, a barman and a US sheriff marshal in Oklahoma, before becoming an actor. He starred in over 400 low budget westerns from the 1910s onwards, and in the early days he also wrote and directed many of his own films and did all his own stunts. Buck Jones proved to be Tom Mix's successor and was a huge draw at the box office from the 1920s right through until after his death in the 1940s. Standing at exactly 6 feet tall, Buck Jones spent much of his youth on a ranch in the Indian Territory of Oklahoma where he learned how to ride and shoot. He served in the US army and worked with a rodeo show and a circus, before moving to Hollywood where he initially played alongside Tom Mix. After a number of years, he established himself as a leading man who was always dignified, brave, and ready to do battle with any bad guy who came in his way. He had a horse called Silver who rode with him throughout his adventures. During his heyday in the 1930s, Buck Jones was among the most popular stars on the big screen, and at one point in his career he was receiving more fan mail than anyone else in show business.

William 'Hopalong Cassidy' Boyd, Charles 'Durango Kid' Starrett and Johnny Mack Brown were among the other cowboys who stopped off at the Assems to water their horses and shoot some bad guys. It was always rumoured that when Johnny Mack Brown's films were showing at the Assems, he would stay in the Imperial Hotel across the road and park his horse around the back by the Holy Trinity. Roy Rogers and Gene Autrey were the singing cowboys and they were well liked too, although the crowd got a little bit impatient when they burst into song. However, one thing that wasn't tolerated at all was romance. 'The boy' often had a leading lady, and there would be uproar when he turned his attention to her instead of shooting the villains. If 'the boy' gave a girl a peck on the cheek the crowd would stampede out to the toilets like a herd of wild cows, but if they heard shooting they'd all run back in again. There were more gunfights outside on the Mall afterwards. It was always said that if a person passed the Assems when the crowds were coming out it was easy to tell what kind of film they had seen. If it was a cowboy picture everyone would be shooting each other with their fingers, while if it was a swashbuckler they would be fencing with invisible swords.

THE STAFF OF the Assembly Rooms acquired a mythical status not unlike the personalities that appeared on the big screen, and

The Legendary Georgie O'Sullivan.
Courtesy of Mary Murphy

none was more famous than a man who hailed from the Old Youghal Road called George O'Sullivan. He was a low sized pleasant man who worked as an usher in the Assems for most of his life, and was a beloved character to all those who went there. The only uniform he had was a hat, and he was one of the general handymen who had to attend to all the tasks that might arise during a days work. Armed with just a silver torch, he organised the queues outside, kept the peace inside when fights broke out, and tidied up afterwards when the film was over. During one show a member of the crowd saw Georgie walking behind the screen, and suggested he was going into the picture to clean up after the shoot outs. From that point on, whenever a bad guy was killed on screen, the crowd would roar out 'Georgie, remove the body!' That tag line followed him every where he went. According to his daughter Mary Murphy, when he went to football and hurling matches the crowd would chant 'Georgie, remove the body!' if a player was floored in a tackle.

Georgie's partner in crime was a tall thin man who was nicknamed Slim Somerville after a cowboy in one of the westerns. Like Georgie, he was a law and order man who had his own methods for sorting out the queues to ensure the blackguards didn't gain admission. Tim Daly from Victoria Avenue was a regular visitor to the Assems in the 1930s and 1940s, and he recalls seeing Slim taking the law into his own hands. If someone started messing in the queue, Slim would move him to the back of the line. He did this with the knowledge that the house would be full by the time the troublemaker got to the top again. When denied admission, the angry fellow would turn to Slim and burr 'I'm a coming for you Slim – and I'm a coming gun heavy'. As if Georgie and Slim didn't have their hands full dealing with outlaws and 'hard chaws', on one unique occasion they had to display their talents as real life cowboys too. According to David O'Keeffe from Blarney, one day a farmer and his workers were driving a herd of cattle down the South Mall to Marsh's sales yard when the wayward cows wandered through the high arched doors of the Assembly Rooms. They had quite a bit of difficulty getting them out again, and afterwards Georgie had more unpleasant things to remove than bodies.

Miss M.E. Spencer was one of the long standing managers of the premises, having taken over the job in the 1910s and remained in place until the 1940s. Her family were originally from the Fermoy area and were related to the late Princess Diana. Along with a lady called Miss Rawling, she was the chief cashier who sold the tickets to the hundreds of hungry film fans. Timmy Linnane from Douglas Street was the chief operator, and his brothers Willie and Mossie worked as projectionists in the Lee and the Pav respectively. Timmy became the last manager of the Assems before it closed. The very distinctive

Timmy Linnane

Goodwin Family from Gardner's Hill were the owners of the cinema, and they maintained an air of grandeur in the place. When the Goodwin sisters were selling the tickets, they dressed in the style of Marlene Dietrich, with a matching 1920s style pull down hat.

As the owners were members of the Protestant faith, they closed the cinema every Sunday and supposedly used the hall for bible readings that day. However in the 1950s, it became commercially necessary to show films on those evenings. Shortly after their introduction, a supernatural presence started to make regular appearances in the cinema. According to Richard Murphy whose father Humphrey worked as an usher in the Assems, the ghost of an old sea captain first appeared immediately after the showing of films on Sunday night. His journey began at the operating box at the rear of the auditorium, and from there he travelled along the western hall to the ticket box in the foyer. On reaching that point he would ascend the stairs to an office on the first floor, which was occupied by the First Mutual Building Society. When the captain reached the door of that office, the noise of his footsteps ceased. One evening a service man from Western Electric was working on the projectors in the operating room, when he heard the door to the box opening and closing, and he sensed footsteps behind him. When he looked around and found there was no one there, he was so alarmed he left quickly and refused to return to the Assems ever again. Meanwhile, the ghost continued to make his presence felt every week until the cinema closed.

IT WAS IN DECEMBER of 1964 when the end finally came to the Assembly Rooms. A huge hall showing films on the cheap in the middle of the South Mall could scarcely make enough money to survive during a period of economic buoyancy, and it became apparent that the Assems would have to find alternative tenants if they wanted to stay around. Georgie had retired his torch a few years earlier and went on to pursue a career as a gardener, while the youngsters who had cheered and booed the great westerns of the 1930s and 1940s had grown up and moved on. On the final night, Saturday the 19th of December 1964, a double feature consisting of *Sword Men of Siena and Cairo* were the last pictures to be screened. James N. Healy, the famous Cork theatre personality, bought the last ticket and was presented with the key after the show. Silence then descended on 22 South Mall, and no clamour or excitement would ever grace those premises again. The Assems was later bought by the Capuchians who intended to use the place as a community centre, but these plans never saw the light of day. Subsequently the demolition men stepped in, and the building was knocked in 1970. Only the elegant yellow brick exterior was spared by the ruthless wrecking ball.

THE IMPERIAL

"Go in crippled, come out walking"

ON SATURDAY AFTERNOONS, hundreds of children would walk past the Palace on MacCurtain Street heading for the Coliseum on the corner. The Palace displayed stills in the window for the pictures that were on show, and Kathy Daly who worked there as a cashier remembers how some of the children would stop and look in to see what was on offer. One afternoon a young fellow turned to his friend and said of the show in the Palace 'That's a big boys one. We'll go down to the Col and if the Col isn't any good we'll go down to Miah's.' Miah's, as the Imperial Cinema on Oliver Plunket Street was known, was truly the end of the line for most people. For many others it was a no go area, known only by its ferocious reputation.

The building that was once home to the Imperial Cinema

The word Imperial usually conjures up images of grandeur, opulence and unparalleled splendour. When one thinks of the Imperial Hotel on the South Mall, all these lofty images spring to mind. For a cinema sporting the same title, one would expect the Queen herself had parked her royal posterior there at one time or another. Yet if the use of irony had ever been employed in the naming of a cinema, then the Imperial was a classic case in point. It was anything but majestic. The Palace cinema might have been imperial, but the Imperial certainly was no palace. Located in the same building that today houses the fashionable men's clothes shop Savilles, the Imperial was a perfect example of a traditional fleapit. Small, squat and lacking in any sort of creature comforts, it is perhaps not surprising that many of the movie going population of Cork decided to discard its pretentious name, and instead opted to call the place after an individual who once had the pleasure of being its most famous and prominent employee – Miah.

The man after whom the cinema was named was Miah, the long suffering commisionaire. He was a distinguished looking man of average height, with wavy white hair, gold rimmed glasses, and he was immaculately dressed for the occasion. He was the ever present figure, always at hand to take care of any of the problems that might arise. Miah was a popular figure amongst the Imperial's clientele, but the crowd enjoyed taunting him too. On any given night when the film was nearing its climax, the crowd upstairs would shout out the first line of the nursery rhyme 'Who killed Cock Robin?'. The reply from downstairs was 'Miah!'. This was known to provoke the man into action, and so the chanting would continue with 'And who watched him die?' until the lights in the auditorium came on and Miah himself charged in to put a stop to it. Blackguarding of this nature happened all the time, and it was for this reason that the cinema became known as Miah's.

IN THE FIRST DECADE of the 20th century, the movies as a medium of mass entertainment were in its infancy, and the venues that were used to screen them were often of a temporary nature. Hundreds of makeshift movie theatres called 'nickelodeons' sprang up around America to cater for the huge interest that the public showed in moving pictures. They were built in converted storefronts and charged a nickel admission. The Imperial was originally created as such a venue and no one expected it to last for over forty years. Looking back, it's a miracle it lasted for forty days. It opened on Friday, February 7th 1913, at nos. 43-44 George's Street. The building was constructed in the 19th Century and had housed the Munster Co-operative Stores Ltd. in previous years. When the Imperial took up residency, it was only the fourth venue to operate as a place for screening moving pictures in Cork.

In its first weeks, it provided one continuous show from 3pm to 11pm daily, and charged the prohibitive prices of 1s for the circle and 6d for the stalls. In the early days the Imperial billed itself as *'Cork's Premier Picture Theatre'* and *'The Finest Cinematograph Entertainment in Cork'*. Such a claim may have been justified at the time as it did provide a wide variety of the most recent films that were on offer, sometimes showing as many as six films during a show. (Bear in mind that the running time for a film back then was 10 to 15 minutes). *Kings of the Forest,* a classic wild life film was among the attractions that drew large crowds in the first weeks the cinema was in business. This was a particularly fascinating picture for the majority of spectators who got to see exotic animals like lions and tigers in motion for the first time. However, one lady who went along to the Imperial shortly after it opened was very confused by the experience, as she had never seen a moving picture before. The beam from the projector caught her eye and she stared at that for a while trying to make out the images, until one of the ushers came along and told her she might see the picture better if she turned around and faced the screen.

Over time, the Imperial lost its title of *'Cork's Premier Picture Theatre'* and plummeted from a lofty position at the top of the list of Cork's places of entertainment to a spot firmly rooted at the bottom. The reasons for this were many as we shall see. While the quality of films and cinemas improved in the 1920s and 1930s, the Imperial's standards didn't move with the times. They found their market by appealing to children and those who couldn't afford the prices of the larger cinemas. By the 1930s, it cost just 10d then to sit in the balcony, while those who sat downstairs had to pay 4d. Cheaper prices meant more customers, and at that time queuing to get in was a long, arduous and chaotic process. Ex army men Michael Farrally and Owen Gorman worked there as doormen, and they were well able to control the crowds. Often the unruly queues couldn't fit on the footpath and spilled out onto the street, but back in those days there was little traffic to worry about. Seamus Quinn who lived on Oliver Plunket Street was often allowed out to go to the 7 to 9 show on a weekday. He recalls that "The Imperial was rough, ready, and had a hardy crowd going in. You queued up and you got a bit scrunched going in and you wailed in the queue and you swayed, and if you were small you got crushed and if you were big you were crushing the small fellows."

The balcony was considered to be the most luxurious spot inside the house and there was always a mad rush to get to the best seats. Those 'armchair' seats were cushioned and laminated, but they had a hollow centre to them that caused embarrassing noises when someone sat down. One of the main reasons they were installed was because the material in them was flea repellent. No cinema in Cork had a higher population of fleas than the Imperial. Some people referred to the place as Lourdes because if you went in crippled you'd come out walking. Because the seats upstairs were that bit more expensive than downstairs, the 'aristocrats' who could afford them would often start a holy war if anyone else lay claim to their precious territory. However comfort came at a price, and the main drawback to sitting in the balcony was that the ceiling was so low down, there was always the danger of hitting one's head. In parts it was so steep that a person had to twist his neck sideways if he wanted to get a good view of the picture.

Downstairs was much more basic. The screen was just inside the main entrance, and the seating consisted of about twenty long wooden benches where people were crammed in like sardines. If a tough boy arrived late and all the seats were taken, he would push his way onto the bench rather than stand for the whole picture. The misfortunate individual who was sitting on the opposite end of the row usually ended up being shuffled onto the floor. Unfortunately, sitting downstairs brought all sorts of other hazards as well. The rowdy bunch who could afford the more expensive seats upstairs would often throw whatever they could find down on the unsuspecting individuals who were not sheltered by the balcony beneath. Frankie Hayes from Albert Road went to Miah's one night when he was just a young fellow in the early 1940s. He was forbidden from going in there because of its bad reputation, but he defied authority and went in all the same with a gang of his friends. They were watching the film downstairs when all of a sudden an almighty commotion erupted a few rows in front of them. "Loads of people jumped up and started moving about. Everybody was wondering what was going on, and then we saw that this fellow was taking a leak over the balcony. Some guy underneath got soaked and shouted up to yer man 'Would you ever wave it a bit. I'm saturated!'"

LIKE THE ASSEMBLY ROOMS, the films shown in the Imperial were usually cheap B movies, but all that mattered for most people was getting in to see a picture. The programme usually consisted of two funny short films, followed by a trailer or two and then a double feature. The main films were usually a black and white western, a gangster picture or a war movie. Charlie Chan murder mysteries were also very popular. Each Chan show featured the wise oriental detective and his 'honourable number one son' unravel a crime that appeared to be of ridiculously complex proportions. Of Chan's great problem solving abilities someone once said "We were all trying to think how he figured it out and we thought it was awfully complicated, but then some of us wouldn't have seen a hole in a ladder." Even if the films were second rate the audience expected good entertainment, and if the programme didn't meet their expectations there was hell to pay. No screen in Cork was pelted with more objects, and it was often torn, burned by cigarette butts or stained by disgruntled customers. Regardless of the damage, the show always went on – even if that meant showing a film on a screen with a six foot gash down the middle.

The Imperial's projection box was small and confined like the rest of the cinema, and it was accessible through the men's toilets which were considered to be the filthiest in Cork. Those who worked in the box had a lot of problems to contend with, and they were regularly distracted by messers who made their jobs all the more difficult. The switch for the house lights was inside the auditorium, and one of the operators had to come out to turn them off at the beginning of each show. Of course no sooner had he done that than someone would come along and turn them on again. The projection hatch through which the films were shown was located downstairs at the rear of the cinema, and many a person standing at the back or going out to use the toilets would put up their hands and block the beam. More imaginative patrons stepped in front of the hatch and made faces and charades that were cast onto the screen. Noel C. Ryan from Cathedral Road remembers how some 'hard man' always interrupted the film at most important moment. "Something exciting would come on in the film and everyone would be waiting, and then someone would put his hand up and block the hole." This led to all sorts of pandemonium, chaos and of course 'colourful' language.

With all these distractions, it's hardly surprising that there were so many breakdowns. Dick Donovan was the chief operator, and Derry Seymour and Jack Drummy were his assistants. They often had to contend with films that arrived in poor condition. The reels were often cracked and scratched, and the splicing frequently broke, throwing the auditorium into darkness just as the picture was getting interesting. As they waited for the film to return, the crowd would start stamping their feet and roaring 'We want our money back!' This was followed by Miah rushing into the auditorium with a stick which he would whack off the front bench (usually empty because it was so close to the screen) and shout 'Quiet!'.

The crowd rarely responded to Miah's commands, yet as the 1950s approached, another kind of silence descended on the premises. By then people had more money in their pockets and no longer had as much need for places like the Imperial. Improvements in public hygiene meant that the fleas which had so long been a part of the experience were now gone, but by then so were most of their customers. They showed their final film on Saturday, July 3rd, 1954. It was a Technicolor western called *Montana Territory* starring Lon McAllister, Wanda Hendrix and Preston Foster. Many of the Imperial's employees went on to find work in other picture houses around town, while the building was sold off and was taken over by the Hanover Cycle Company. By today's standards the Imperial may not have had much to offer, but in those days it provided a world of entertainment that kept legions of people amused.

5. AROUND THE CITY

SUBURBAN CINEMAS STARTED springing up in the neighbourhoods around Cork almost as soon as moving pictures first started to grab people's attention, and they managed to hold their own for many years. The Northside had a monopoly on suburban movie houses in the early years of the 20th Century, and while they didn't match the city centre theatres for elegance and style, they certainly made up for it in personality. There were three in total – St. Mary's Hall facing the North Chapel, the legendary Lido on the Watercourse Road, and the Cameo on Military Road opposite the entrance to Collins Barracks. The latter was a cinema that had its beginnings in the silent days but achieved its greatest notoriety in the 1960s and 1970s. The first two offered a 'modest' service to their customers, but the Cameo in its time was the best equipped cinema in the city. Each had its own following, and all contributed to the rich tapestry of entertainment that Cork had to offer.

ST. MARY'S HALL

IN CORK'S LARGE FAMILY of cinemas, St. Mary's Hall was essentially the black sheep as it was never officially recognised as a picture house. This was in spite of the fact that it showed films for more than thirty years. Built around the turn of the 20th century from red brick with Bangor slates, it was located at the bottom of Cathedral Road facing its owner and administrator, the North Chapel. It originally functioned as a community centre, and in its early years it was used as a gymnasium and as the home to the 'League of the Cross' temperance society, known to the locals as 'de leg of de cross'. An organising committee of local residents oversaw its running, and in 1912 they decided to put on a season of moving pictures. The building had to be altered to accommodate the new machinery that was required for screening films. When the first pictures were shown on Monday the 21st of October 1912, all the expenses were justified as throngs of people from all over the city converged on the Hall. On its opening night a total of nine one reel films were presented, including the raunchily titled comedies *What the Window Cleaner Saw, Farmhouse Romance* and *Married Lovers,* as well as the serious dramas *Aviator V Autoist* and *The Dove and the Serpent.* In its first years as a cinema, the Hall showed films six days a week except on Sundays, and admission was charged at a the princely sum of 6d and 3d. A local pianist called Miss Griffin provided the piano accompaniment to go with the pictures.

St. Mary's Hall

Michael Murphy, who worked as a projectionist in the Palace for over fifty years, lived almost next door to St. Mary's Hall in his childhood. As a reward for singing in the Cathedral choir, he received a free pass for the cinema from Herr Aloys Fleischmann Senior. This was before the advent of sound, yet in an age when the projector was subject to frequent breakdowns, the crowd would offer plenty of spectacular sound of their own. Many of the films of the time were two reel comedies or westerns, and Laurel and Hardy, Charlie Chaplin and the cowboys Colonel Tim McCoy and Ken Maynard were always a big draw. Despite being owned by the North Chapel, the Hall was often a lawless place. According to the eminent local historian Timmy Ryan, in the latter days of silent films a violinist was employed to provide the background music, but the misfortunate individual spent much of the night trying to fend off all the objects the crowd was throwing at him. Another man was later brought in to provide protection, but he got even more abuse. Both of those people were relieved when a top of the range American sound system was installed in the early 1930s. The first talkie to be shown there was the Wheeler and Woolsey comedy *Dixiana*.

In addition to their cinematic activities, St. Mary's Hall also contained a Savings Bank that allowed people to put some money away for the rainy day. The Penny Bank as it became known, was originally started by Bishop Coholan during the First World War for the purpose of raising money to invest in war bonds. The Bishop was a controversial figure among his flock as he had strong Unionist leanings. This made him quite unpopular with many of the more Nationalist community in the North Parish. When he excommunicated Republicans from the Church during the War of Independence in 1920, someone retaliated by hurling a bomb at the Hall which blew a big hole in the roof. Even after it served its original function, the Penny Bank continued to operate for many years. It received most of its business from the local children, although nobody ever managed to save all that much. Noel Magnier who came from Gerald Griffin Street invested his money in the penny bank as a child, but like so many others he never had the patience to let it grow in value. "People would save a penny on a Friday and probably withdraw it on the Monday, much to the chagrin of the management."

THE HALL WAS a great place of amusement for children from the Northside in the 1920s, 1930s and 1940s. It was a time when work was scarce, wages were low and families were large, yet when people went to their favourite picture houses they left all their troubles at the door. Films were shown nightly at 7pm and again at 9pm, and they held just one matinee each year on St. Stephen's Day. The programme changed twice a week, and while most of the pictures that played there were B movies, the audiences were often treated to reissues, short films and the ever popular 'following up ones'. The auditorium was divided into three sections, and as in all houses, the least expensive seats were the two penny hard benches up at the front. Behind that on a gentle incline was the soft bottomed 3d section, which was separated from the front by a brass rail. The balcony was the preserve of courting couples, doctors and members of the 'local aristocracy'. Charging a King's ransom of 6d, most people could never afford to sit up there.

Most programmes presented at that the cinema consisted of a double feature of a western and a drama. The bulk of the crowd at the 7 to 9 show were made up of young people going along to enjoy the action of the old west, while a more mature audience would attend the later show for a piece of more sophisticated entertainment. Jimmy O'Regan and Dickie Doyle were the chief operators, and people were always curious to know how they managed to squeeze two films into a two hour show. Noel Ryan, who was an apprentice operator in the Lee during the 1940s, often travelled up to the Hall to borrow some of their short films which were in scarce supply during the war. One night he asked the chief operator how he was able to run a double feature from 7 to 9 and again from 9 to 11. Speaking in a glorious Cork accent, the man replied: 'Tis like this boy: in the first show we show's all the cowboy picture and we drops two reels out of the society picture. Then at the second show we drop's two reels out of the western and we shows all the society picture.'

Michael McCarthy who lived nearby, and who spent twenty five years of his working life in the Pavilion, was a regular patron of the Hall in his younger days. "We lived for the cinema because it was the only thing we had." It was also the only entertainment that most people could afford, and even then they had difficulty raising the price of admission. "We'd be all day trying to get the money. Sometimes you'd be lucky to have it and other times you'd have to go begging for it, selling jam jars and that sort of thing." Mr. Murphy and Mr. Hayes were the main ushers, and it was said that Mr. Hayes was the more sympathetic of the two as he would often let two people in for the price of a 2d ticket. However, if someone tried the same trick with Mr. Murphy he was as likely to throw them out as let them in. As Michael McCarthy said, "With the crushes going in, you'd be trying to keep to the right hand side so that when you'd get your ticket you'd go in past Mr. Hayes." If the Hall was full, people would go down Shandon Street and spend their hard earned money on a bag of chips that came wrapped in the Echo. The chips were quickly devoured, and when they were finished, people would squeeze the paper to get every last drop of vinegar out of it.

Women with shawls are now just a part of Cork's history, but in the bygone days they were a regular feature of the City. The shawls were long heavy garments worn around the shoulders. Because of their length they were very useful for the purposes of smuggling. Jerry O'Riordan from Blackpool recalls the days when he and his friends would stand penniless outside St. Mary's Hall in the hope that one of the 'shawlies' would turn up, as they had a unique method of getting people in. "You were sound if you knew the one," he said. The women would buy their ticket and walk in to see the picture, but there would often be three pairs of legs coming out from under the shawl. Because the ticket box in the main foyer had a very high counter, the seller couldn't see all the different pairs of feet underneath. Many was the person that risked life and limb and a possible expulsion from the hall trying to sneak in that way, but no one ever got caught or evicted despite the fact most of the staff knew what was going on.

John Corkery was the manager of the premises, and as secretary of the Hall's committee in 1912, he was one of the people

Johnny Corkery

responsible for starting its tradition of showing films. A well remembered and well liked figure in the Northside, Mr. Corkery came from Redemption Road and for more than thirty years he ran the picture house and the Penny Savings Bank. He was always present to monitor the crowd, and he had his hands full trying to control the scampering activities of the younger patrons. As those who were caught misbehaving were immediately ejected, it was hardly surprising

that he became a very unpopular man in certain circles. One person whose feathers he really rattled was a character best remembered in Cork as 'The Rancher'. The Rancher (whose real name was Owen McCarthy) owned a box car and travelled the streets of the city selling wooden blocks and advertising himself with the slogan 'Burn my blocks and have hell on earth.' Such was his familiarity to the public of Cork that one year he was put up as a candidate in the local elections. He only managed to poll sixteen votes, despite the fact that his extended family alone consisted of over thirty people. In response to his poor showing, he composed 'The Rancher's Curse':

> *May all my relations and many others,*
> *Be early clients of O'Connor Brothers,*
> *May Johnny Corkery of St. Mary's Hall,*

Be blown away by a canon ball,
May blondes and brunettes who think they're smashers,
Get pimples and boils from Connie's Rashers,
Nine times champions but never again,
Up the Barrs and shag the Glen!

IN 1943 THE local curate, Fr. Thomas O'Keeffe, was made a Canon and became administrator for the North Parish. He oversaw the running of St. Mary's Hall and would often turn up before the show dressed in all his official vestments. It was under his reign that the church decided to off-load the premises. In the late 1940s, the Hall was sold to the company of Capitol and Allied Cinemas, who bought it with a view to continue running it as a picture house. The last film shown under the church's ownership was the religious epic *The Song of Bernadette* starring Jennifer Jones, and such was the public demand that it was one of the few films that ran there for a full seven days. The poster for that film was still on display weeks after the cinema had closed. The new owners had plans to extend the premises, but the presence of an ESB substation immediately behind the Hall made this move difficult. Their petition to have it removed was rejected, and as a result the plans to improve the building fell apart. The Hall lay silent for the remainder of the 1940s, and it was subsequently sold on to the Corporation who knocked it a few years later during a period of extensive development in that area. Noel Magnier recalls "I remember going in when it was being demolished and we were rummaging around for mementoes." The demolition crew had done too good a job and sadly they weren't able to retrieve anything.

THE LIDO
Shoot-outs at the Ranch

FOR HUNDREDS OF people who grew up around the Northside, the Lido Cinema on the Watercourse Road is a place where many of their happiest childhood moments were spent. Located in the very same building where O'Meara's Camping Store traded up to a few years ago, it was without doubt the most famous and best loved of all the suburban picture houses, and its happenings over the years have been converted into local legend. It served largely the same community as St. Mary's Hall, but as it was a little bit more sophisticated, people had to learn their trade in the Hall before they could graduate to the Lido.

The old Lido Cinema

On Monday the 2nd of November 1920, The Blackpool Cinema was the first picture house to open on that site. Incidentally, it was the same day as the Lee Cinema opened on Winthrop Street. While it was a boom time for the cinema business, it was a very

110

troubled time for the city of Cork. The Blackpool's original opening was scheduled for the previous week, but owing to the death of the Lord Mayor Terrence MacSwiney in Brixton Prison, it had to be postponed. The whole city entered into a period of mourning and all places of entertainment closed their doors for the next seven days as a mark of respect. When the projectors rolled for the first time the following week, the Blackpool drew full houses with a film called *Sporting Life.* This picture, which contained footage of a boxing match and a horse race, drew loud cheers from an enthusiastic audience who may as well have been watching the real thing.

The building was owned and operated by Mrs. Hussey from Cobh, who also lived on the premises. In addition to showing films, the Blackpool hosted live shows, political rallies and Irish dancing competitions. They advertised themselves in the most glowing terms and claimed to have the most comfortably fitted and well ventilated auditorium in Cork. This was an ever so slight exaggeration of the truth and as the City Engineer's report for the Public Health Committee in 1926 indicated, in its early years the Blackpool didn't even adhere to the basic standards that were required for a public entertainment venue. The report read "This application is out of order as no lighting is installed, exit notices defective and seating not fixed or spaced." As a result, the Blackpool was initially refused a licence to serve as a public entertainment venue. Several months later, having failed to bring the place up to scratch, the application was withdrawn and the Blackpool Cinema was closed down.

AFTER LYING VACANT for a number of years, the building at 70-74 Watercourse Road was acquired by a Dublin man called Eddie Coghlan in the early 1930s. It was he who gave the place its more familiar name – the Lido. The new picture house was decorated in an atmospheric Venetian style with a grand painting of a gondola on one of the walls, and it was fitted with all the latest projection and sound equipment. It came into being on Sunday the

25th of October 1931, showing *Wild Company* as its first film. The Lido had two shows a day at 7pm and again at 9pm, and they had a change of picture three times a week, on Sunday, Monday and Thursday.

Mr. Coghlan, the owner and manager, was a low sized man with glasses, and he ran the cinema for over thirty years. He was known as 'the shadow' as he was very skilled in catching people who were trying to duck from the cheap seats at the front to the more expensive ones at the rear. According to Noel Magnier, a regular patron of the Lido, "He would literally appear out of the shadow hence the nickname. Just when you thought it was okay to get into the dearer seats, out would step Mr. Coghlan and a hand would be on your shoulder and you'd be escorted out firmly but fairly." He employed the services of ushers Florrie Wallace, Jim Dowdall and Tom to help him maintain law and order, and they stalked the aisles like marshals from the old west. Members of Mr. Coghlan's family also worked there, including his daughter Ruth who later married the famous Cork composer Sean O'Riada.

Everyone from Gurranebraher, Spangle Hill and Blackpool went to the Lido, and it became central to the lives of many people from the Northside for many years. Each evening the crowd queued up in Berwick Lane at the side, and there would be great rowdiness and excitement as they waited to get in. The place was nicknamed 'the ranch' because of all the westerns they showed, and throughout the picture everybody would roar, stamp their feet and pretend to shoot at the bad guys. After the film was over the mayhem continued outside where people acted out what they had seen on the big screen. There were always fights over who'd get to play which part as everyone wanted to be 'the boy', and they'd all try to out do each other with their daring and bravery. Pat O'Neill from the Northside remembers seeing one of his friends rolling off the roof of a shed and onto the ground after pretending he'd been shot. After he got up, he dusted himself off and carried on as before. Of course they made them much tougher in those days.

OF ALL THE attractions the Lido had to offer, the best remembered were the serials, or as they were known in Cork, 'the follow up wans'. A saga consisted of fifteen or twenty episodes of about twenty minutes in length, and one instalment was shown every week. The 'following up wans' featured all kinds of virtuous heroes like Flash Gordon, Buck Rogers, Captain Marvel, Superman, Batman and the Phantom, who battled villainous mad doctors, spacemen and other monsters. Each episode ended with the hero getting himself into a fix where escape appeared impossible, and just as it seemed as though he was going to be killed, 'Continued Next Week' appeared on the screen. Despite the seemingly overwhelming odds, the hero always managed to evade disaster and emerged unscathed to fight another day. Serials became one of the mainstays of film production in the silent era, but with the advent of sound the bigger Hollywood studios turned their attention to the more lavish productions and left the serials to the smaller production companies. It seemed as if they were as doomed as the hero who was left hanging off the side of the cliff, but in truly dramatic fashion they managed to escape and find new life as entertainment for children.

Jerry O'Riordan from Blackpool was first taken to the Lido by one of his brothers in the 1930s when he was very young. By the time he reached the age of seven he started to go by himself, and *Flash Gordon* was the big attraction of the day. The actor in the lead role was the former Olympic swimming champion Larry 'Buster' Crabbe, who also played the part of Buck Rogers. Monday evening at 7pm was the night the new episode would first be shown, and everyone was anxious to see whether Flash Gordon was killed or escaped from the clutches of the evil villain Ming. When he got away, Flash always managed to get himself into another fix by the end of the show. The conclusion of each episode was greeted with booing and hissing from the crowd who would then have to wait a whole week to see how things turned out. Jerry didn't always have the full price to get in every week, so he had to go to great lengths to make sure he had enough money to see the next chapter. "We'd be outside the Lido and we'd have three half pennies in our hand. The Lido was two pence. Come hell or high water, we'd be an hour and a half outside before seven o clock begging for the half penny to get in." Sometimes he was lucky, and other times he wasn't. Each episode of *Flash Gordon* began with the humming of spaceships, and if he heard the humming while he was still trying to get the last half penny, he knew he was too late that week.

Getting in to see the follow up one was very important, because if you missed one episode you might not get the chance to see it again. Pat O'Neill was a dedicated follower of the serials in the 1950s, and religiously went along each week. "The one that sticks out in my mind was *The Phantom*. There were fifteen episodes and I followed it up all the way through, and I was going up for the fifteenth episode and I accidentally slipped and banged my head off the ground and I had to go home. Therefore I missed the ending." The final episode never came back and he never got to see how the story was resolved.

THE PRICE OF the Lido was never terribly expensive, but like Jerry O'Riordan, many a person had to improvise for the few pennies. The selling and trading of jam jars was one of the most popular ways of getting the money for admission. Before the new episode of 'the following up one' or the latest western, people from all over the Northside raided the cupboards at home in search of empty jam pots and glass bottles. It wasn't always easy to get a hold of these items as many people used them for storing something else when they were empty. Those who were lucky enough to get their hands on one would wash and clean it, and then exchange it at the confectionery firm of Ogilvie and Moore in Parnell Place. They paid a half penny for a small pot and a penny for a big one, and the money was then used to get into the picture. When glass was in short supply, the Lido accepted jam jars and bottles directly as payment for admission. Mr. Coghlan gathered all the containers that people brought in and then traded them in turn.

While some people were thrifty and resourceful in gathering together the money for the Lido, others operated a series of schemes ranging from daring to ingenious in order to get inside for nothing. One seemingly foolproof scheme involved using the same ticket to get two people in. When you'd buy your ticket from the kiosk, the manager would take half of it before letting you inside. People would then go in and take their seats, but sometimes they might slip the remaining half of the ticket out under the door to someone who was queuing up outside. That guy would then take the stub and walk up the steps and into the foyer. He'd show the ticket to Mr. Coghlan and say that he had just gone out to get sweets in the shop next door. As Mr. Coghlan had seen so many people coming and going, he usually didn't question them too much and so that scam worked as often as not.

There was one final 'racket' which was employed when nobody had enough money, but this was only used in the event of a real emergency. Timmy Ryan who grew up in the Northside tried this method on a few occasions. "If we hadn't the money we'd be all standing outside against the wall. A fellow would come over and he'd collect all the pennies and he'd go in and he'd sit at the edge of the seat down at the door nearest to the screen. At about quarter to eight he'd bang open the door and you'd have to run in. Everyone would scatter all over the place in between the seats and everything." Some people always got caught, but enough got in to see the film for nothing.

While the Lido often had more 'free' customers than paying ones, the management took pride in their business and occasionally attempted to make the place a bit more high class. The grand city centre cinemas employed ice cream girls who walked the aisles during the intermissions selling their products to the customers, and one time the Lido tried to follow suit. They hired a girl, gave her a tray, a bicycle lamp and let her loose on the crowd. Someone would call her over and ask to see an item on one end of the tray. While she was showing it to him, another person would sneak up at the other side and grab as many sweets as he could without getting caught. Noel C. Ryan from Cathedral Road witnessed the poor girl doing her best to sell her wares. "She didn't last long. She went down one end, and when she came back the other end there was nothing in the tray and she didn't make a penny." Other times some brazen young fellow would tip over the tray and there would be a free for all to grab the stuff. It was a place where only the toughest survived.

FIGHTS WERE NOT uncommon in a cinema like the Lido, and there was always a rough element involved with the place. Much of the rowdiness was innocent enough, but over the years it got steadily worse. By the 1960s, the cinema had a very bad reputation and this was seriously affecting its business. Troublemakers were barred, but usually they would have to commit a very serious crime before that happened. One person was barred for life after he set fire to the Echo and tried to push it through the letter box. The Lido received its final blow on April 9th 1962, when an individual was stabbed during a show in the cinema. That was the final straw for the management, and on the April 14th 1962, the Lido shut its doors after its last film, *Good Sam,* which starred Gary Cooper.

Several weeks later the outside of the building was painted in dual shades of light and dark blue, and a new name adorned the wall at the side – the Palladium. The Cork hotelier Paddy Coughlan bought the premises and converted it into a new upmarket cinema, which opened with *Three Coins in a Fountain*on on the 21st of June, 1962. The new 450 seater cinema was lavishly decorated with plush comfortable chairs, and the auditorium was equipped to cater for stereophonic sound. Although it showed a full programme seven days a week, and it was the first venue in Cork to show Sunday matinees, within three years of opening the Palladium's days of business were concluded. Despite all the fanciful efforts to revive interest, this small suburban picture house could simply not survive the pressure of the television age. After forty five years of service as a picture house, nos. 70-74 Watercourse Road closed quietly in 1965.

The cinema following its renovation in 1962. Courtesy of Irish Examiner

THE CAMEO
"New York Standards in Cork"

THIS ELEGANT THEATRE which was located on Military Road opposite Collins Barracks, had a long and eventful history both as a cinema and a dance hall. Built on the sight of the old Garrison Hotel, it originally opened as the Bellevue Cinema on September 23rd 1920, under the ownership and management of Mr. Michael Prendergast. Showing films continuously each evening from 6pm to 9.30pm, the Bellevue quickly became a popular haunt for the locals, and it was a favourite retiring spot for the British troops stationed in the barracks across the road. General Strickland, the commander of the British forces in the South of Ireland during the War of Independence, was even known to enjoy an evening watching a film in the balcony. Despite a few years of prosperity, the Bellevue was converted into a dance hall in the mid 1920s as the owners thought that this line of business would be more

The Cameo Cinema. Courtesy of Seamus Quinn

profitable. The venue was renamed the Gaiety Ballroom, and over the next four decades it became one of Cork's ballrooms of romance. It was part of a series of dance halls that was owned by the aforementioned Mr. Prendergast, who also had the Gresham in Maylor Street and the Arcadia on the Lower Road. It wasn't until 1964, at a time when most of the old picture houses were closing, that the place was resurrected as a cinema.

THE STORY OF the Cameo is essentially the story of Seamus Quinn. In a career that spanned thirty five years, he worked as an operator, a manager and an owner, and was acquainted with every technical and commercial aspect of the cinema business. Born and bred in the heart of the city, he picked up the cinema bug at the age of eleven when he bought a 9.5 mm pathescope silent projector and reels of silent 9.5 mm film from Mayne's Pharmacy on Pembroke Street. He built his own miniature cinema and screen at home, and at a later stage installed a sound system for his own private viewing pleasure. It seemed as if moving into the business professionally was the next logical

Seamus Quinn

step, and he went on to become an apprentice operator in the Pavilion in 1948 at the age of fifteen.

After a few years in the job he became restless and felt that he was getting nowhere. "If I was going to get promoted it was going to be if someone left which they didn't – in projection rooms they don't leave – or if they died." At the age of twenty one he headed for England where he finished his training as an operator. While there he worked with the Grenada Group and the Gaumont Group and learned more in six months than he had in the restrictive atmosphere of the Pavilion's projection room in nearly six years. He rose through the ranks of the Gaumont Group quite quickly and became the head operator in Leighton. In England he was able to run the show by himself, and the money he was receiving was far better. In Ireland he was getting just £4 17s 6d a week as the fourth operator in the Pavilion, while the head operator was getting between £25 and £30. By comparison, in England he was collecting a weekly wage in the region of £80 to £100 when he was still in his early twenties.

After staying in England for four years, he returned to Cork in the mid 1950s and set up his first cinema in Sarsfields Court near Glanmire. He bought a shop and a car garage and he converted the latter into a cinema by lengthening it, widening it and installing a 16mm projection system. He named this 130 seater picture house the Cameo. In the days before television, he also ran a travelling cinema circuit to areas where they didn't have much access to cinemas such as Ballincollig, Berrings, Coachford, Killeagh and Lady's Bridge. The Cameo in Sarsfields Court was a successful venture and he later installed two 35mm projectors. The place was full regularly and people came in from town. "The whole thing was a drug. What started as a hobby turned into a business." He also operated a hackney service, mostly driving staff from the Sarsfields Court sanatorium in an out of town, but on Saturdays he would also ferry the children whose parents didn't own cars to the matinees in the Cameo. For this service he charged a few extra pence. After a number of years down there he decided to sell the business and he moved to town in 1964. "It was a toss up between buying the Gaiety Ballroom in St. Lukes or the Temple Michael Dance Hall. I decided it was more viable to take on the Gaiety because you were in the city."

He bought the premises from Mr. Cant who owned the Coliseum, and Mr. Coghlan who had been the proprietor of the Lido. When Seamus moved in, he found the original screen from the days when the place functioned as the Bellevue Cinema. It was a square screen with rounded corners made from a cloth material, and it had been used as a backdrop for the dance hall. When he opened the Cameo in December 1964 it was used primarily as a venue for adult ballroom dancing, but after acquiring a cinema licence he decided to return to his roots. The newly restyled picture theatre opened on April 18th 1965, with *Barabbas* starring Anthony Quinn, and he used the old projection equipment from the cinema in Sarsfield Court. He intended the premises to function as a cinema on weekdays and Saturdays, and revert to a dance hall on Sundays. He even designed his own seats which, depending on what the place was being used for, could easily slide on and off the floor.

AT FIRST THINGS moved slowly, and the Cameo's business as a cinema was poor. Never one to lie down and admit defeat, Seamus Quinn realised that if he was to make a go of the cinema the best thing to do was to renovate the whole building and fit it out with the most modern equipment. He personally constructed and installed a panorama screen 41 feet long and 18 feet in height, which was curved to give the greatest picture size possible, and he also altered the projection room to fit the new machinery. Originally the box extended beyond the façade of the building (like in the Lee Cinema), but it was reduced in size when it was converted to a dance hall in the 1920s. By September of 1967 things finally started to go right, and the new Cameo Panorama Cinema opened with a screening of *The Magnificent Showman*.

The 1960s was a decade when many other cinemas were closing, and some of those that remained in business were showing their age. Despite this, the Cameo set new standards of comfort and technical superiority. Seamus spared no expense in fitting out the premises. He went to Manchester to pick out the high back 'teddy bear' seats, and Seekers of London supplied the gold flame proof drapes for the walls. He first put in a 35mm projection system, and later a 70mm system, and in 1974 it was the first cinema in Cork to

Inside the Cameo. Courtesy of Irish Examiner

install Dolby Sound. It had New York standards in Cork. "We were geared for everything. Everything they had in London or New York I could show in Cork." He had standby equipment to replace any item in the projection or sound system in case something malfunctioned, and he also had a generator to cover the eventuality of a power cut. "The show always went on. We never lost a show." The sound system was of such a high quality that people often arrived early to hear the music that was played before the beginning of the main film.

The Cameo started showing reissues of mainstream films in its early days, but it was more specialist and offbeat pictures that really brought the place into its own. Unusual films like the Italian documentaries (or as some called them shockumentaries) *Mondo Cane* and *Africa Addio,* and the Swedish drama *Elvira Madigan* really established the cinema's reputation. Most of these pictures were foreign, often they were soft pornography, but all had been passed by the censor. His main distributor was a small company in Dublin called Independent Films. "I always made plenty of money from their films because I sold the films like they never sold them. I made a big thing of them on the paper. I spiced up the ads and made them big and people didn't even know they were the same films as downtown. When these films were shown in the city centre cinemas the newspaper ads were in ordinary print, but I used to put illustrations around them – bras and knickers and things like that. A bit of suggestion and re-styling." The style of advertising grabbed people's attention and brought them to the Cameo out of curiosity. The high standards of the presentation along with the comfort and good parking kept them coming back.

Seamus always looked for films that would run for an extended period of time, and a spicy Italian picture called *Malizia* became the biggest success in the cinema's history. The film was a comedy about a sexy young woman who goes to work as a housekeeper for a widower and his three sons. She starts to lead the father on and becomes the object of desire for all of his children. *Malizia* (the Italian for Malicious) was a huge money spinner, and people were coming from as far away as Waterford and Tipperary to see it. The film ran for many weeks, and when he brought it back again at a later stage, it pulled in huge numbers second time around too.

As many of the Cameo's films were of an adult nature, the policy of the house was over 21s. Seamus ran a very strict ship and he was always on the door himself to check the crowd that was going in. Because everything on the premises was top of the range, the audiences were expected to comply with his rules and he was not going to allow anyone to treat the place as a halfway house.

Most people accepted his standards, yet if trouble did arise it was dealt with swiftly. "I remember one night there was a group came in – they were respectable people too – they might have had a few jars but they looked all right to me and I passed them. They were fellows and girls and couples and there were seventeen of them altogether. They started this carry on and I went back to them two or three times and I said 'Listen lads, is it going to stop or isn't it, because there's a few hundred people in and there's seventeen of you and I'm telling you now if you don't stop you'll have to go.' So it quietened down for two or three minutes and it started again. I took off the dress suit coat, I kicked opened the panic doors and I phoned up Pat [his son in the operating box] and told him to stop the show and put on the lights. I put out seventeen. Now they went out – but they could have mangled me. I was really cross about the whole thing as there was never a disturbance in the place before that. They left and they all lost their £2.50 a seat – all seventeen of them. But that was it and a big applause went up." After that no one else dared to test him.

RUNNING THE CAMEO was a full time job for Seamus, and he took charge of every aspect of the business. "I was the projectionist, I was the boss, I was the owner, I was the bouncer, I was the lot.". Despite taking the lions share of the work, he retained a small staff, including his son Pat, to help him run the show. Pat was just a boy when he started in the business, and Seamus taught him all the tricks of the trade. Today Pat is the head projectionist in the Reel Multiplex in Ballincollig, as well as the chief operator for the Film Festival. Other staff members included Kay Boland, Declan Lynch and his wife Celia. Declan had worked as an operator in many of the Cork cinemas including the Assembly Rooms, the Lee, the Pavilion, the Ritz and the Lido, and he was one of the most skilled projectionists in town.

To ensure that the Cameo drew good crowds, Seamus was obliged to offer different and innovative services. In the 1970s, many of the films on general release were for an over 18s audience, and there was a shortage of wholesome entertainment for a younger crowd. This prompted him to hold matinees of cartoons and the like on weekends. These sessions proved sufficiently popular to warrant the setting up of a children's cinema club in 1972 which screened three hours of films on a Saturday afternoon exclusively for kids. The shows were always noisy and colourful like the old days in the Assems, and they were well supported. The Cameo was also the first cinema to introduce late shows in Cork. They ran from 11pm until about 3am on Fridays, Saturdays and Sundays, and brought in big crowds all the time. Other cinemas subsequently followed, but the Cameo still managed to retain their customers. One Easter, Seamus screened *Jesus of Nazareth* in conjunction with all the convents in the city. It was a huge success as the nuns wanted all their pupils to see this film, and they bussed them in from miles around. However many of the pupils had no interest in watching a lengthy biblical epic and they spent the time smoking and talking out in the hall.

IN 1975 SEAMUS SPREAD his wings further and opened the Classic on Washington Street. He tried to run a cinema similar in style to the Cameo, but it never took off. He sold it after a few years, but he continued to keep the Cameo functioning for a while longer. Unfortunately, the lack of quality films proved to be an insurmountable stumbling block, and in October of 1983 he decided to convert the premises into a modern discotheque. Although the projectors occasionally rolled when good pictures became available, things were slowly falling apart and by 1985 the Cameo's film showing days were over. Seamus had created blueprints to convert the cinema into a five screen multiplex many years before the Capitol became the first such venue in Cork. The plan was to bring the film from the bigger screens all the way down to the smallest until it was milked. He had designed the projection rooms so that a single copy of the film could run from one cinema into another without interruption. This innovative measure depended on all the machines operating simultaneously, but sadly it never came to fruition.

After the cinema closed, Seamus continued to use the building as a disco and a second hand furniture shop. He also ran a pirate radio station named Sunshine Radio out of the operating box which launched the career of 2FM DJ Michael Cahill. He finally left in 1990, and after a decade of lying vacant, the Cameo was eventually knocked and an apartment complex was built in its place. Despite the fact that it is now gone, the Cameo still remains a key element of Seamus Quinn's psyche. "I still dream about the Cameo and it will be a part of my will that the day I'm going I will ask them 'please take the hearse that way.'"

The Cameo's final days. Courtsey of Seamus Quinn

6. THE LAST PICTURE SHOW

THE CINEMA INDUSTRY in Ireland suffered its most severe blow at the end of 1961 when the Irish television station RTE was established. It made its first broadcast on the 31st of December that year, and as a consequence, the cinema business would never be the same again. Although cinemas had battled for a long time against spiralling operating costs and the burden of entertainment tax, the introduction of television in Ireland was the final blow. While the national figure for cinema attendance in 1962 was 35 million, by 1987 it had reached the lowest ever point with just 5.2 million people going to the movies. Things had reached a very low ebb and consequently the once beloved picture houses of Cork started to become a thing of the past.

Although St. Mary's Hall ceased its film activities in the 1940s, and the Imperial on Oliver Plunket Street departed in the 1950s, most other houses in the city continued to thrive until the early 1960s. At first the impact of television didn't seem all that severe, except to Paddy Kearney the ticket tout who found that he couldn't sell overpriced tickets on a Sunday night any more. However, none could ultimately escape the wrath of the new medium. Many dedicated moviegoers viewed the new technology with derision and named it the 'idiot box'. People complained about the lack of quality programmes and argued that the uniqueness of the cinema experience was something that couldn't be affected by television. Unfortunately this was not the case, and by 1964, two of the longest serving picture houses in the city succumbed to the undiscriminating hand of progress. The Coliseum, the first cinema to be built in Cork back in 1913, was the first to go.

The Col's enforced closure was due in part to the advent of television. Southern Coliseums Ltd, who owned the cinema, refused to sell the premises as they harboured a hope that the tables would turn for the better within the film industry. The cinema was scheduled to reopen in 1965 with the MGM musical *Till the Clouds Roll By,* however that plan ultimately failed to materialise. The building was later bought by the G.P.O. who used it as the sorting office for many years, and it was subsequently resold to a leisure company who converted it into the bowling alley and amusement arcade it is today.

In December of 1964 the Assembly Rooms surrendered to the same fate. Without so much as a warning, the oldest cinema in Cork shut its doors on Saturday the 19th of December, 1964. Several months later, Frankie Hayes and Mossie Linnane went into the Assems to look at the projection equipment on behalf of a priest from Passage West. The place had not been cleaned since its final show, and was in a complete state of disarray. "The Echo from the closing night and sweet papers were all still on the floor, and the smell was shocking" according to Frankie. In addition the screen had been torn. It was a sad and rather undignified ending for a cinema that had such a celebrated history and had served as one of the most popular venues for thousands of Cork people for over fifty years.

Other houses around the country were feeling the pinch as well. In a meeting of Irish Cinemas Ltd in 1965, it was noted that audiences were continuing to decline in all parts of Ireland, but the worst hit areas were Cork, Limerick and suburban Dublin. It was expected that an increase in wages, rates and advertising, in conjunction with a fall in audiences, would result in further closures. Out in Hollywood, the old studio system was also falling apart, and many of their new films failed to capture the public's imagination. In an attempt to win back the crowds in Cork, some cinemas started resurrecting popular classics from the 1930s and 1940s. In the mid 1960s it was not uncommon to see an old Humphrey Bogart gangster film or a John Wayne western playing in the Capitol or the Ritz.

BY THE 1970s, the future looked exceedingly bleak. Most homes in Cork had a television, and going out to the pictures was low on many peoples' list of priorities. Choices of films on offer were frequently poor, and all the cinemas suffered as a result. The Savoy was the first to be hit. In July of 1973, Mr. Gerard P. Harvey the managing director of Odeon Ireland, Ltd decided to close the grand movie theatre, citing the collapse of the film industry as the reason. On Saturday, February 1st 1975, after more than four decades in business, it showed its last film at a gala night in aid of the Film Festival. The final night at the Savoy included a stage show featuring cast members from the popular television show *Upstairs Downstairs,* and the Irish premiere of the all star disaster movie *The Towering Inferno.* The live performance was badly rehearsed and went down like a lead balloon, but this seemed scarcely relevant to those who turned up to say goodbye to a beloved Cork institution. It hit the staff harder than anyone else. The Savoy employed more than any of the other cinemas, and many of those who worked there had devoted a lifetime's service. The manager Ms. Renee Ahern locked the premises after the film had finished and crowds had left, and then there was darkness in the Savoy. It reopened later in the year to house the Film Festival one last time, but after that it was closed for good, sold off and converted into a shopping centre.

If the 1970s had been the blackest period for cinema on record, the 1980s were even worse. The arrival of videos allowed people to watch the latest movies in the comfort of their own home just a few months after they hit the big screen, and Cork Multi Channel was being piped into increasing numbers of houses, giving people plenty of alternative entertainment. Just six cinemas remained in Cork – The Palace, The Classic, The Pavilion, The Lee, The Capitol (along with The Mini Capitol), and The Cameo. Seamus Quinn, the owner of the Cameo, decided to shut up shop in the mid 1980s due to a lack of business, and things were not much better for the city centre cinemas. Their day in the sun had passed and those old theatres were starting to show their respective ages. Frequently the cinemas would only open the stalls or balcony for a show, as the crowds were simply not there to warrant the opening of both. The writing was on the wall and the decision was clear: cinemas had to reduce in size and cost if they were to survive.

When the Palace closed in 1988, the end was really at hand. The magnificent auditorium on MacCurtain Street that opened as Dan Lowrey's Music Hall ninety years earlier, showed its final film *Planes, Trains & Automobiles* on June 4th of that year. Fergal Crowley went there in the week it closed and saw a whole way of life coming to an end. "I remember going to the Palace the week it closed to see *Planes, Trains and Automobiles.* Up to that the ushers and usherettes would have their uniforms, but this time the usher was wearing just a sweater and trousers...I got talking to him and some of the girls and sympathised with them about the closing of the place, and they were in bits really." However, the Palace was sold to the Everyman Theatre Company and was converted into a theatre once again.

Abbey Films, who owned the remaining cinemas in Cork, recognised it was time to take effective action against the escalating costs and financial hardships of running bulky, outdated theatres. They had kept many of the old cinemas going for as long as possible, but by the end of the 1980s these houses were no longer financially viable. It was time for a major change in the industry, so in 1989 Abbey Films decided to convert the Capitol into a six screen multiplex. The Pav, the Lee and the Classic continued to operate for several months until the new complex was ready, but as the Capitol's conversion neared completion the Pavilion was closed. Several days later the Lee followed, and on the night of August 10th 1989, the Classic was the last one to go. The age of the individual picture house had truly come to an end. However, there was a poignant coincidence in those final days that defied all logical explanation: the last ever film to be shown in an old cinema was *Mississippi Burning,* and the central characters in that picture – like the directors of Abbey Films – were named Ward and Anderson.

7. PHOENIX FROM THE ASHES

IT WAS A SUNNY Friday afternoon in the late summer of 1989, and hundreds of people were waiting patiently on the pavements of the Grand Parade for the arrival of the caped crusader in Cork. Batman was the master of disguise, the enigmatic hero who battled seemingly impossible odds and always emerged on top. Despite many scrapes with doom, he always defeated the bad guys in the final reel and restored order to the world. Batman's arrival in town was symbolic of the changing fates of Cork's cinemas. The 1989 film version of the legendary comic book hero was heralded around the globe as one of the most spectacular films of the decade, and it drew huge crowds in every city which had a picture house big enough to screen it. No doubt a film of this nature would have elicited a similar reaction amongst the people of Cork on any other day, but Friday the 11th of August, 1989 was extra special. It was the day the new Capitol Cineplex opened its doors.

The Capitol Cineplex in 2003

131

The Capitol was the first such cinema of its kind in Cork, and it was apparent to any passer-by on that Friday afternoon that this venture would prove as popular amongst the new generation of movie goers as the other cinemas had been in the past. The Lord Mayor of Cork, Counsellor Chrissie Aherne, opened the new 1,100 seater Cineplex on its first night. It was the most modern cinema in the British Isles at the time, costing £1.75 million to construct, and it came fully equipped with all the trappings of a new state of the art multiplex. The crowds that gathered for the grand opening were on a scale that hadn't been seen in Cork for many years. Fred Hill, who had been in charge of the old Capitol, and Donal Kelly, who was the boss of the Pavilion, took over the management of the new complex. Many of the old staff who had dutifully worked in the other cinemas were re-employed in the Cineplex.

The prohibitive economic costs of sustaining the old cinemas became unfeasible by the late 1980s, and the only way for the business to survive was to open multi-screened cinemas in one building. This not only kept the operating costs down (as well as the admission prices), but it provided a venue that was perfectly suited to the tastes of the new generation of cinema goers. And they came in droves. For the first few weeks getting into the new Capitol was as difficult as getting into Fort Knox, and the crowds would continue to come. In the years that followed, it was not uncommon to pass the Capitol on a week night and see 'House Full' signs posted in the foyer. When big films came to town, like *Jurassic Park* in 1993, or *Titanic* in 1998, the queues would stretch to Patrick Street on one side and Oliver Plunket Street on the other. The 'good old days' had clearly returned.

The success of the Capitol inevitably led to the opening of additional multiplexes around the City. Cinema World, a custom built five screen venue opened in Douglas in the Summer of 1994, and this was followed by the Reel in Ballincollig in 1997. The Kino opened on Washington Street in the Autumn of 1996 to cater for a more selective line of continental and non mainstream movies, and in October 1998 the six screen Gate Multiplex at the North Gate Bridge joined the line up. With current talks of an eleven screen complex due to be built in Mahon, it seems as if going to the pictures has once again become a fashionable thing to do. Despite all the threats from television, video, DVD and satellite movie channels, nothing has managed to replaced the thrill of sitting in a darkened movie theatre and watching a great drama play out in spectacular manner on the big screen.

The Kino on Washington Street

The Gate Multiplex

133

IN 2000 THE GRAND CIRCLE of the Savoy was redeveloped as a glamorous new night club. However, for much of the previous decade this site had been vacant and had fallen into a state of disarray. The ceiling sporadically leaked, dust accumulated in every corner, and paint flaked off the walls. The remains of a leisure centre lay unused and decaying where once a couple of hundred cinema goers had sat. Apart from a few fading wall decorations and the relics of the ornamentation that circled the screen, there was little to remind people of what once stood there. However, following the restoration in 2000, the Savoy has become one of the most glamorous entertainment spots in Cork yet again. The downstairs section was converted into a shopping centre in 1977, and was modernised in 2001.

The Grand Circle of the Savoy in 1999, prior to its renovation

The Pavilion is currently home to the HMV music and video store. The facade has not been altered significantly, and if you look closely at the HMV logo at the top, you can still make out the faded letters PAVILION behind. Upstairs, the decorations of the old restaurant remain, but it is unlikely that any of the hundreds of people who pass through have any idea of what it used to be. At the rear, in what was once the auditorium, is a fashionable night club which for many years traded under the name The Pav. The Palace has been converted back into a theatre and so enjoys live performances in much the same tradition as Dan Lowrey's Palace of Varieties did over one hundred years ago. Since 1990 the Col has been a bowling alley and amusement arcade, but an ornate mosaic footstep saying COLISEUM still exists at the entrance, denoting the building's illustrious past as a cinema.

The entrance to the Coliseum

The Assembly Rooms has retained its elegant exterior, but the main hall was demolished many years ago and the St. Francis Workshop was built in its place. For a number of years there was a restaurant on that site called the Assems, and in 1995 it hosted an exhibition celebrating the films of John Wayne and other westerns that were the cinema's main attractions half a century earlier. Sadly the restaurant closed in 1999. The Lee on Winthrop Street currently lies vacant awaiting a new lease of life, and the Lido in Blackpool is also empty and deserted. An elegant men's clothes shop on Oliver Plunket Street called Savilles is now home to what was once the infamous Imperial Cinema. Although Miah's has been gone for nigh on fifty years, on occasion older people still wander in and fondly remember the way things used to be. Meanwhile the Ritz, St. Mary's Hall and the Cameo have been torn down to make way for the future...

IF THE SQUALOR OF Miah's is a thing of the past, so too is the glamour of the Savoy. While Cork has transformed itself from a provincial town at the forgotten end of Ireland to a bustling city of European culture, many of its most distinctly individual features have also disappeared. The filmgoers of today can walk into a multiplex in any city in the Western World and see the same films in largely the same conditions. There is nothing unique about their experiences. Cinemas have become yet another consumer item. It is to be used, enjoyed and then thrown away. A younger generation raised on a life of plenty will never fully appreciate a trip to the pictures the way their parents and grandparents did. It meant so much more to the older generations when they had so few material comforts to keep themselves amused. The pictures were their great escape. They were the place where people could relax and unwind and forget their troubles for a few hours. Whatever the weather, be it hail, rain or snow, people battled every condition to get to the pictures. As Michael McCarthy, an usher in the Pavilion for twenty five years, put it so eloquently: "It was easy to satisfy us. We lived for the cinema. Cinema was our life. When you went out for a night you went out to the cinema. The usual talk was 'What picture has come to the Savoy? What picture has come to the Pav?'" The passing show gives us all just a few moments of glory and wonder before we are shuffled along and our place in the spotlight fades into darkness. Only now in memory do the cinemas of old continue to exist and entertain, but the memories burn as brightly as ever.

ACKNOWLEDGEMENTS

Many people assisted me in the writing of this book, and I must pay tribute to them for all their help and advice. There are three people in particular who require special mention: my mother Anne, my father Eamonn and my aunt Meta O'Mullane. Sadly my mother died some time before the book's completion, but it is to her memory this work is dedicated. My father's stories of the old cinemas fuelled this book in its early days, and he gave me great counsel during the years I was writing it. My aunt Meta worked tirelessly on my behalf to ensure that this book finally made it to print, and was always encouraging and supportive during the difficult times.

I am very grateful to the following people who played their part in the genesis of this work: Alan Collins, Coleman Doyle, Maura Curtain, Neil O'Brien, Brian O'Mullane, Noel and Siobhan Corbett, Michael Cahill, Laura McCormack, Margaret Dowling, Claire Kelly, Bernadette O'Driscoll, Terrie Burke, Denis Dinan, Noel Dunne, Janice Volk, Kristian Chantry, Christine Deasy, and everyone who worked in Cinema World, Douglas in 2002.

Thanks also to Kieran Burke and the staff of the City Library; Kieran Wyse and the staff of the County Library; Brian Magee and Michael Higgins of the Cork Archives Institute; Derek O'Gorman, Deirdre and Connor from St. Francis Workshop; Fr. John Collins of the North Parish; Fr. David Murphy of St. Patrick's; Patricia O'Sullivan of the Everyman Palace Theatre; Billy O'Mahoney of the Savoy Shopping Centre; Eddie Mullins of Saville's Clothes Shop; The Irish Film Centre; Anne Kearney, Paul McCarthy, Pat Good, Aidan Forde, Ann Forde (retired), Donal Coughlan (retired) and Colm O'Connor of the Irish Examiner for their permission to allow me to reproduce photographs from their archives.

AUTHOR'S INTERVIEWS AND CORRESPONDENCES

When writing a book of local history, the most important source of information is usually peoples' stories and reminiscences. This project began with the aid of Mr. Michael Murphy, whose entire working career was spent as an operator in the Palace. He gave me some of the many facts and figures I needed to get this book started, and pointed me in the right direction to find out all the other details. I am immensely grateful to Mr. Donal Kelly who provided me with so much information about cinemas in Cork that I could have written several books. I would also like to thank Mr. Pat Mulcahy who is perhaps Cork's foremost film fan. This book would not have been possible without their considerable contributions.

Many former cinema employees greatly helped me in the writing of this book: John O'Leary (Capitol), Seamus Quinn (Cameo), Michael John O'Sullivan (Lee), Leo Ward (Abbey Films Ltd.), Dan Williamson (Savoy), Andy Condon (Savoy), Fred Hill (Capitol), Frank & Marie Nash (Coliseum), Noel Ryan (Savoy & Lee), Barry Leahy (Palace), Kathy Daly (Palace) & her husband Tim, Michael McCarthy (Pavilion) and his wife Pat, Stanley Cant (Coliseum), Eamonn Coughlan (Capitol), Denis Burke (Capitol), Declan Lynch (Cameo), Paddy Buckley (Coliseum), Marie Linehan (Savoy), Robert McDonald (Savoy), Dan Hyde (Capitol), Anne Broderick (Palace), and Phil O'Donovan, Mary Murphy, Richard Murphy, and Finola Power who supplied me with stories of their parents' experiences in the business.

No book on Cork cinemas would be complete without the memories of their customers: Timmy Ryan, Fergal Crowley, Jerry O'Riordan, Noel C. Ryan, Pat O'Neill, Eddie Cummins, Noel Magnier, Frankie and Fran Hayes, Joe Daly, John O'Shea, David O'Keeffe, Liam Hurley, John Kenny, Hilda Buckely, Donal Cronin, Martin Linehan, Dan Leahy, Donie Gleeson and Eileen Arnold. I offer my sincere apologies to anyone I forgot to include. Your contributions were greatly valued nonetheless.

SOURCES

Author's Interviews and Correspondences
The Cork Examiner
The Cork Weekly Examiner
The Evening Echo
The Cork Constitution
The Irish Times
Inside Cork
Cork Hollybough
The Corkonian
Guy's Almanac and Postal Directory
The Kine Year Book
Middle Parish Chronicle
Everyman Palace Restoration Programme
Public Health Committee Engineering Report 1926
'The Duke Rides Again: Remembering the Assems' – St. Francis Training Workshop
'Is That You Boy!' – Noel Magnier
'Spangle Hill Forever' – Dave McCarthy
'The Way We Were' – Declan Hassett
'Media Memories of Cork' – Roy Hammond
'Echoes at the Fountain' – Jim McKeon
'Irish Cinema – An Illustrated History' – Brian McIlroy
'Cinema & Ireland' – Kevin Rockett
'The Companion to British and Irish Cinema' – John Caughie & Kevin Rockett
'My City by the Lee' – Richard T. Cooke
'The History of the County and City of Cork' – C. B. Gibson
'The Burning of Cork City' – Soughgate Books
'The Story of Cork' – Sean Beecher
'Who's Who in the Movies' – Leslie Halliwell
'Leonard Maltin's Movie and Video Guide' – Leonard Maltin
'The Guinness Encyclopaedia of Hollywood'
www.imdb.com

4371291